The example of B
spurred me on tow,
His words, fleshed out through his own real life
experience, are an inspiration to all Christian singles to live prayerful and Christ-centered lives. He
provides practical helps as well as spiritual motivation to maximize our singleness for God's glory,
as we believe God for His best in all areas of life.

Lisa Weglewski
DIRECTOR OF WOMEN'S MINISTRY
FOOTHILLS BIBLE CHURCH, LITTLETON, CO

I am delighted to comply with your request to write
a brief commendation of your book *Believing God for
His Best*. Your reference to the way that God in His
sovereign and scriptural leading brought Stephen
and me together—in a marrage that has now lasted
over 56 years—makes me exclaim, Hallelujah! I remember his sharing with me the revelation God had
given him from the Word, and how meticulously
he followed those instructions, until God brought
me into his life. My prayer is that as this chapter is
read, hundreds of young people will be led away
from the tragic marriages they might have become
involved in to the marrage that God intends for
their lives. The tragedy of divorce amongst Christians
today breaks my heart; and I trust that your book
will go a long way to resolve this problem. May
God bless you and your written ministry.

B. Heather Olford
STEPHEN OLFORD CENTER FOR BIBLICAL PREACHING

I welcome the privilege of writing a few words concerning my good friend Dr. Bill Thrasher's new book, *Believing God for His Best*. Nothing is more needed in our contemporary Christian world today. With the tangled marriages, broken homes, and divorce rates, one wonders what can possibly be the solution. Needless to say, the only one is returning to God's blueprint as recorded in His Holy Word. I am grateful that he has drawn on the experience of how God brought my sweetheart, Heather, and me into the vital union of marriage, now going on our 57th year! It seems inconceivable that God would initiate such a sacred ordinance as the marriage of a man and woman without giving instructions on how He plans to bring this about to fulfill His glory, as well as His purpose, not only in mutual pleasure, but in bringing precious little lives into a Christian home, and then a full spiritual life. For this reason, I congratulate him on his book in general, and the privilege of having our names included in his treatment of this delicate, but important subject in the hour in which we live. May God grant the book a wide readership, especially amongst our young people.

Dr. Stephen F. Olford
STEPHEN OLFORD CENTER FOR BIBLICAL PREACHING

BELIEVING GOD *for* HIS BEST

How to
Marry
contentment
and
singleness

BILL THRASHER

MOODY PUBLISHERS
CHICAGO

© 2004 by
BILL THRASHER

Library of Congress Cataloging-in-Publication Data

Thrasher, Bill, 1952-
     Believing God for his best : how to marry contentment and singleness / Bill Thrasher.
          p. cm.
     Includes bibliographical references.
     ISBN 0-8024-5573-5
     1. Single people--Religious life. 2. Thrasher, Bill, 1952-
I. Title.

BV4596.S5T48 2004
248.8'4--dc22

                                        2004006194

1 3 5 7 9 10 8 6 4 2

Printed in the United States of America

*Dedicated to every single who desires to
maximize their time of singleness
for the Lord and discern God's wisdom
in regard to a marriage partner.*

*Dedicated to every caring parent who desires to
protect their children from scarring
their lives before marriage and
shepherd their children to wait on God
for His will, person, and timing
for a marriage partner.*

*Dedicated to every caring person who desires to
honor Christ by esteeming singles
and esteeming marriage.*

CONTENTS

Foreword   9
Introduction   13

1. Seeing Singleness from God's Point   19
   of View
2. Waiting on God for a Mate   25
3. Finding God's Provision on the   31
   Other Side of a Temptation
4. Repenting of Idolatry After   39
   Experiencing Love at First Sight
5. Rebirth of the Vision: Purify My Heart   45
   Amidst Closed Doors
6. Experiencing God's Providence and   51
   Delayed Answers to Prayers

7. Learning from the Other Side   63
of the Story

8. Developing a Conviction Before God   73

9. Discovering the Secret of Contentment   79

10. Making an Important Commitment   87

11. Pondering a New Direction   97

12. Handling Your Passions   105

13. Discerning God's Will   113

14. The Secret of Waiting   125

Notes   131

Appendix 1: Questions to Consider   135
and Explore

Appendix 2: Vows   141

Study Guide   147

FOREWORD

THE CHRISTIAN CHURCH, with its ubiquitous pro-family and pro-marriage emphasis, unwittingly constructs an idol to which many Christian singles fall prostrate.

Dr. Thrasher exposes this idol and deftly offers advice on how to tear it down.

The idol is marriage.

Marriage is an unexpected idol because Scripture holds it in such high regard. But, Dr. Thrasher explains, when a person believes marriage can quench those thirsts of the heart meant only for Christ to quench, that person has made marriage an idol.

Sadly, this marriage idol is alive and strong within the church. Many singles truly believe they cannot be content without a spouse. I myself fall into this trap at times. As a single minister, I am subject to constant heckling and inquiries from fellow pastors and laity alike. I am frequently encouraged toward marriage (sometimes with specific suggestions of a prospective mate), and people are eager to know the latest inflection of my heart. While these comments and questions are usually playful or offered in my best interests, they reflect a general attitude in the church that a man (or woman) is not complete until wed.

I am convinced that countless single men and women can relate to this pressure, and our families are often the greatest offenders! I recently heard of one wise church leader who advised his spiritually volatile son that what he needed was a wife, as if marriage would settle his spiritually wavering heart. It seems there are very few problems a single person faces to which someone does not think marriage is part of the solution. This is sad, and it causes many unmarried people to make an idol of marriage.

Holy matrimony is designed by God, promoted by God, and blessed by God. It can be a beautiful reflection of His glorious gospel (Eph. 5:32). But the Bible does not treat it as the universal elixir able to cure any ill that plagues a single person.

Rather, the Bible teaches that God is good and in complete control of all things. Hence, whether a believer is single or married, he can rest knowing that he has God's best. This truth is the key to true contentment. Knowing that God has me single for a reason, I am free to pursue Christ and His Kingdom with my whole heart.

This is precisely the message that Dr. Thrasher delivers in this unique book. He masterfully dismantles the marriage idol while still holding marriage in high esteem. Weaving together his own fascinating biography, rich biblical exposition, and eminently practical advice, his book speaks from the heart, to the heart.

Dr. Thrasher deals a devastating but gentle blow to the marriage idol, and his message needs to be heard. If you are single, I encourage you to read *Believing God for His Best* and to examine your own heart to see how you may be making an idol of marriage. *Believing God for His Best* will also help parents, siblings, pastors, and friends of single people to rethink their emphasis in discussing marriage.

My prayer is that the church would read and heed Dr. Thrasher's words. Perhaps we, like Dr. Thrasher, can be pro-family and pro-marriage without tempting singles to make an idol of marriage.

James Seward
PASTOR OF SINGLES AND YOUNG ADULTS,
COLLEGE CHURCH IN WHEATON

INTRODUCTION

TO SINGLES

PENNY AND I were married at ages thirty and thirty-six. I, Bill, was the older one. We agreed together that we would always hold singles in high esteem. We are indebted to the Lord for the things that He did in our lives during our many single years.

Our hearts' desire is that God would use this book to encourage each single person to grow closer to Him in his or her singleness. The length of time that a person will have this opportunity will vary. Whether you are high school age, college age, or a mature adult, God has a plan for your singleness.

We know that there are times when the church does not champion the positive role that singles can and do play in the Lord's plan to build His church around the world. May you sense the Lord's great delight in you as His son or daughter whom He dearly loves, even in your most challenging moments.

While no two stories of how God guides a person to his or her spouse are the same or necessarily should be the same, it is our desire to share our lives with you. This book contains more autobiographical sections than any I have written. My wife's and my desire is to share from our hearts what we have learned about God's esteem of singleness, the importance of scriptural convictions, the secret of contentment, practical aids to living in purity, and principles to discern God's will as you wait on Him and His timing.

We do not pretend to say that this process is always easy or without pain—it was not for us. We do commend you to a merciful and good God who is willing to meet you at every turn as you present your life to Him and feast on His love and care for you. He does not ask you to repress or deny your longings for intimacy, but He wants you to share your heart with Him. He offers His compassionate and miraculous help for you to live a life of purity in a world that He knows is perverted. May God use this process in your life to build not only a deeper intimacy with Himself but also deeper bonds within key relationships in your life and the Christian community.

TO PARENTS

There is nothing that we are more devoted to than attempting to father and mother our three sons in a way that pleases God. There is also nothing for which we feel more inadequate. We thank God for our parents. At the time of the writing of this book, Penny's mother and father and my mother are still living and have been a great help to us. My father died at the young age of fifty-two. His own father died when my father was a one-year-old. As a result, his father couldn't be a daily role model in his life. However, my father was a wonderful man who gave me one of the greatest gifts that a father can give a son—the gift of his full acceptance.

Whatever your circumstances as a parent, I know that you deeply desire the eternal joy of your children. You would no doubt do anything to keep them from scarring their lives before marriage and to guide them to wait on God for His will, person, and timing for a marriage partner. It is our prayer that God will use this book

to aid you and your children in seeing relationships from God's perspective as you shepherd
them through the moral pitfalls of our culture.

TO ALL

In God's enablement I will pray every day for
the readers of this book to be blessed by Him.
The following is a list of prayers we can pray for
our own lives and our loved ones each week. I was
sent something similar in an e-mail, and I have
adapted it to a prayer for each day of the week.

- *Bless spiritually:* May we know and love You
  as our heavenly Father in such a way that we
  develop sensitivity to Your Holy Spirit and
  hunger and thirst to conform to Your Word.
  Create in us a purifying fear of You that gives
  us a holy joy in abiding in You.

- *Bless emotionally:* May we know You as the
  One who can heal our hurts and remove any
  ground for bondage (such as rejection, failure, resentment, jealousy, and shame). Give
  us the grace to choose to accept Your forgiveness and be a channel of it to others. Give us
  an assurance that You will never fail us and a
  strong hope to believe You for Your promises
  in a way that answers all our fears.

- *Bless mentally:* Guide us to know Your truth and receive Your wisdom. Deliver us from deception and give us godly discernment.

- *Bless personally:* Give us a sense of our value in Christ and favor with You and men. Place in us a vision of Your calling.

- *Bless our relationships with our authorities:* Teach us submission to authorities and direct us to right loyalties, godly soul ties, and wise friendships that encourage us in our walk with You.

- *Bless physically:* Give us Your protective hedge for the safety, health, and strength we need to accomplish Your will.

- *Bless financially:* Give us wisdom to acknowledge You as our Source and Provider. Grant us Your provision and the grace to be good stewards of it.

On a few occasions I have referred to other writings that elaborate on some of the themes in this book for those who desire further insights. May all that is written be used by God to answer the precious prayer of Philippians 1:9–11 in and through your lives. The reference to this prayer is engraved on our wedding bands. May God write it on all our hearts so that His blessings overflow in praise to Him and loving benefit to others:

> *My prayer for you is that you may have still more love—a love that is full of knowledge and every wise insight. I want you to be able always to recognize the highest and the best, and to live sincere and blameless lives until the day of Christ. I want to see your lives full of true goodness, produced by the power that Jesus Christ gives you to the glory and praise of God.* (PHILLIPS)

SEEING SINGLENESS
FROM GOD'S
POINT OF VIEW

CHARLES SIMEON was a pastor in Cambridge, England. For over fifty years, he faithfully served God in this university town and was used by Him to create an environment wherein people could grow. As a result, many from his church were thrust into ministry.

A number of years ago, I heard a series of lectures by Gordon McDonald on the life of Charles Simeon. As a single man at that time, I was struck by Simeon's words:

> I should hate the university above all places if I were a married man. I shall never

marry. In my present state, I am quite a rich man and almost as free from care as an angel. Had I married, I would have had to resign my fellowship and with it my usefulness. I have never felt it a great sacrifice but have appreciated the opportunity to invest in men.

While I did greatly benefit from my own longer season of singleness, I could never fully identify with Simeon's words. Yet they were helpful along with the examples of other godly single men and women who were clearly taking advantage of the practical benefits of their single status.

First Corinthians 7 is a special chapter of Scripture. If it were the only portion of Scripture we considered in relation to marriage, we might come to some wrong conclusions. On the other hand, if we ignore its contribution, we will clearly miss an important part of God's message on this subject.

On three occasions in 1 Corinthians 7 the goodness of singleness is affirmed (verses 1, 8, 26). This is the balancing truth to the general principle that it is "not good" for man to be alone—and thus, the provision of marriage (Genesis 2:18). God, therefore, sees the single state as one of special opportunity because a person's life can be less encumbered with the responsibility of pleasing his or her mate (1 Corinthians 7:32–34) and in this sense more available to the Lord.

A married person cannot function as if he were single. He cannot or at least should not ignore his family responsibilities in order to be available to everybody who needs to be visited or counseled. In this way a person who has no spouse or children can play a more involved role in the life of the church.

The teaching of 1 Corinthians 7 is needed in order to give balance to the subject of marriage. Usually people do not need to be exhorted about the benefits of marriage. This is somewhat innate to the way God has made every person. Making the most of one's time of singleness is the best preparation for marriage in the will of God. Even 1 Corinthians 7 is not attempting to restrain a person from marriage but rather to promote the opportunity in singleness to devote oneself to the Lord (1 Corinthians 7:35).

While I was going through graduate school to prepare for ministry, it was obvious to me that God did not want me to pursue marriage. In my first week of graduate school, my attention was drawn to Proverbs 24:27, which we will look deeper at in chapter 3. While I was resting in the truth that I was now in a preparatory time that allowed my singleness to be an advantage,

I continuously needed this conviction reinforced. The joys and privileges of marriage were obvious, and I was also being reminded that ministries often prefer their positions to be filled with married men. I had to "fight" to rest in the benefits of my present state.

I devoted a day to studying 1 Corinthians 7 in order to realize afresh the advantage of my singleness. After a time of study I took a walk and was praying through portions of this chapter. I quoted 1 Corinthians 7:32–35:

> *But I want you to be free from concern. One who is unmarried is concerned about the things of the Lord, how he may please the Lord; but one who is married is concerned about the things of the world, how he may please his wife, and his interests are divided. The woman who is unmarried, and the virgin, is concerned about the things of the Lord, that she may be holy both in body and spirit; but one who is married is concerned about the things of the world, how she may please her husband. This I say for your own benefit; not to put a restraint upon you, but to promote what is seemly and to secure undistracted devotion to the Lord.*

As I was walking down Swiss Avenue in Dallas and quoting these verses, I looked up at the beautiful sky and pondered the awesome privilege of being able to enjoy undistracted devotion to the Lord who created the universe. This gift is given to all for a period of time and to some for a lifetime.

I later returned to my dorm room and discovered a note from a young lady whom I had noticed that summer. She was asking if I would be willing to take her to the airport. Her godliness and beauty had caught my eye, and I was willing! Momentarily, my meditation of 1 Corinthians 7 was forgotten.

That evening I was a little restless, so I got up to seek the Lord. I had been studying Proverbs and was on chapter 5 of this book of wisdom. I was struck by Proverbs 5:18, which encourages the married man to "rejoice in the wife of [his] youth." I made no connection of this verse to the lovely girl that I would take to the airport the next morning, and after that I would never have any further contact with her. I did, however, make a connection with it to my meditation of 1 Corinthians 7, which led me into a time of worship.

I worshipped God for His beautiful plan. He says that singleness is good and has many spiritual advantages. To affirm the goodness and advantage of singleness is not to deprecate marriage. He also says that marriage is good, and when God gives it, it is to be enjoyed to its fullness.

To affirm the goodness of marriage is not to belittle the exalted state of singleness. I worshipped God that whatever His will was for me in this matter—to be single or married—it was good, acceptable, and perfect (Romans 12:2).

WAITING ON GOD
FOR A MATE

THE COUNSEL that is given in 1 Corinthians 7:27 is to not "seek" to change one's marital status. However, it is also obvious that it is God's will to change many people's status from singleness to marriage, because marriage is indeed His creation (Genesis 2:18–25).

In seeking the Lord, a believer who is single desires not merely to be married but to marry with the full blessing of God. Author Tim Kimmel illustrated entering into the marriage covenant without thinking through what this commitment fully means:

Minister: "Do you take this woman with all her immaturity, self-centeredness, nagging, tears, and tensions to be your wife—forever?"

The dumb ox, temporarily hypnotized by the prospect of being able to sleep with her every night mumbles, "I do."

Then the preacher asks the starry-eyed bride who is all of twenty, "Do you take this man with all of his lusts, moods, indifference, immaturity, and lack of discipline to be your husband—forever?"

She thinks that "forever" means all of next week, because she has never experienced one month of tediousness, responsibility, or denial of her wishes, so she chirps, "I do," in the thought that now she has become a woman.

Then the patient minister parrots, "By authority committed unto me as a minister of Christ, I pronounce you man and wife. . . ."

As he does he prays a silent prayer for forgiveness, for he knows he lies. They are not now husband and wife and he knows that few of them will ever be. They are now legally permitted to breed, fuss, spend each other's money and be held responsible for each other's bills. It is now legal for them to destroy each other, so long as they don't do it with a gun or club. And the minister goes home wondering if there isn't a more honest way to earn a living.[1]

In my graduate school years, I ran across a book called *Silhouettes* by Helen Kooiman. Each chapter tells the story of a woman behind a notable man of God. For example there was a chapter on the mother of Billy Graham, the mother of Bill Bright, and chapters on the wives of such men as Edward Hill and Arthur DeMoss. The chapter that struck me more than any other was the one about Heather Olford, the wife of Dr. Stephen Olford.

I could identify with Dr. Olford's entering the public ministry as a single man. He sought God for wisdom as to how to approach the whole issue of relationships and marriage in a way that maintained his Christian testimony in the midst of his demanding ministry. After doing an in-depth study of the subject, God impressed him with Jesus' reference to Genesis 2 when He was questioned about the whole matter of marriage and divorce (Matthew 19:3–6).

Dr. Olford discovered from Genesis 2 that God's concern is greater than ours in this matter. Adam did not have the ability to analyze what he was missing or what he needed, for he had never seen a woman. It was God who analyzed the need in Adam's life for a suitable companion.

The Lord not only explained to Adam what he needed but also provided the woman to meet his need and fulfill His plan. In Dr. Olford's words:

> When God explained to Adam what was lacking in his life, he must have acquiesced to God's will, or else God would never have imposed a woman on his life, for to have done so against Adam's will would have been an immoral act. God caused a deep sleep to come upon him, and Adam was prepared to rest in the will of God until God awakened him to the right partner. Only while Adam was asleep in the will of God could God create the woman that was suitable for him in every respect.
>
> Then, of course, there was the awakening— God's consummation of the love, courtship and marriage, as it were. When Adam awakened, the woman that God brought him matched him perfectly. There was an affinity of spirit, soul, body, for they had met in God.
>
> As far as I was concerned, this revolutionized my thinking. Having seen this truth, I decided I was not going to do any kind of exploring to find a wife; I was going to sleep in the will of God. And the amazing thing is that when you sleep in God's will, He puts a protection around you. Many young women could have broken into my life between the ages of

twenty-five and thirty, but they were held off while I did the job God wanted me to do.[2]

The remainder of the chapter explains how in the midst of his ministry he met lovely Heather Brown, who was also involved in ministry and pursuing God's will for her life. God not only enabled them to be acquainted through several mutual ministry opportunities together but also provided a providential meeting. Dr. Olford was recuperating in Ireland from an illness and preparing himself for a ministry in Belfast. During this exact time, Heather was returning to her home in Ireland from a time of ministry.

Heather's sister, Lilian, asked Stephen to join her family for a trip to the Belfast docks. That morning he had read Proverbs 18:22 in his devotions: "He who finds a wife finds a good thing and obtains favor from the Lord." Before the convention began where Stephen was to speak, the Brown family planned a day's outing to the beach. For a variety of reasons, only Stephen and Heather were able to go. As they were driving through the beautiful countryside, he began to share his heart about his plans and directions for ministry that God had given him. Then Heather poured out her desires, burdens, and yearning to serve Christ through her music.

Suddenly Stephen pulled to the side of the road and stopped the car. In his words: "The jigsaw puzzle so perfectly matched that it was not funny. We bowed our heads, I found myself praying that God would guide our lives. As I prayed I thanked Him for Heather, for giving her to me, and accepted her by faith, so that I really proposed to her in my prayers. She followed with a prayer and did exactly the same thing. And when she finished, for the first time in five years I kissed a girl, and we were engaged at that very moment."

What on the surface may seem impulsive is really the fruit of a life of godly restraint and waiting on God for His timing and provision.

3

FINDING GOD'S PROVISION ON THE OTHER SIDE OF A TEMPTATION

A DEAR FRIEND, Michael, requested to introduce our wedding by relating to the wedding guests how God had led Penny and me to marry. The process of our relationship is something that he had prayerfully and compassionately observed. I had never heard of such a request to do a "prologue" to a wedding, but I did consent. I even gave him my personal diary that I kept in the close to seven years of the relationship. With his masterful skill as a storyteller, he communicated the story on that crisp November day in 1988. I am humbled by it and how God has used it to encourage others. We have repeatedly been encouraged to put our story in written form over the past fifteen years. The following pages are an effort to obey these promptings.

BIRTH, SALVATION, COLLEGE YEARS, CALL TO MINISTRY

I was "born" in Montgomery, Alabama in 1952 and "born again" in the same city when Billy Graham came to Crampton Bowl thirteen years later. My growth as a Christian was limited in the next years, but God did prompt me to read His Word.

After joining the Air Force Reserve and serving six months active duty, I attended Auburn University but did not know the Lord well enough to allow Him to form my ambitions and plans. There *I* decided to study business and was met with *outward* success of making the Dean's List, joining a good social fraternity, and being elected president at the School of Business as a freshman. Such outward success did not quench the thirsts of my heart. I knew that *inwardly* I was full of fears and anxieties and was not living for Christ and did not even know how to do so.

In December of 1971, I wandered into Buster's room, a fellow fraternity brother. He was the most unusual person in the fraternity. He not only was a Christian, but his express purpose for joining the fraternity was to lead people to Christ. Up to this point in my life I had never met a Christian who took a stand for Christ in an environment where it was not at all popular to do so. Buster's roommate was moving out and so was mine. I requested to room with him, and God used this relationship to draw me into a full surrender of my life to the Lord. This surrender eventually led to a complete change of plans. While I finished my degree in business, I sensed God's clear call into vocational ministry.[1]

SEMINARY AND PROVERBS 24:27

While I wanted to go into ministry immediately, older and wiser men as well as my loving parents counseled me to get training. After working in a local church, I attended Dallas Theological Seminary. In my first week of classes God spoke to me from His Word in my personal devotions. He used Proverbs 24:27 to give me some direction for the next years:

> *Prepare your work outside*
> *And make it ready for yourself in the field;*
> *Afterwards, then, build your house.*

In the book of Proverbs to "build a house" refers to marrying and rearing a family. This verse says that this is preceded by a preparatory time. I deeply sensed that I was to not focus on marriage at this time but instead consider my schooling as years of undistracted preparation. I did not realize that schooling would last as long as it did. After finishing four years of graduate school that led to a master's of theology, I was encouraged to enter the doctoral program, which lasted two additional years in Dallas, and I spent two more years writing my dissertation in Chicago. The Lord used those seminary years to guide me to pursue a teaching ministry, and in 1980 He graciously opened the door for me to teach at Moody Bible Institute in Chicago.

EARLY YEARS IN CHICAGO

When I arrived in Chicago I reminded God of Proverbs 24:27. According to my timetable it was time to "build my house." The transition from living in a graduate school dorm with numerous colleagues and companions to living by myself in a large high-rise apartment was quite lonely. It was an adjustment when I first began to ride the commuter train and sit next to someone for almost an hour and have the other person hardly speak. Where I was raised, if you sit next to someone for an hour, you learn about most of his life. This loneliness compelled me to look to the Lord in a new way. It was a time of experientially learning what it meant to "delight in the Lord."[2]

While I was tempted to enter into a relationship, it was clear to me that my years of being prepared by God were not over. I "married" my ministry and threw my life into teaching and writing my dissertation.

TEMPTATION AND GOD'S PROVISION

God calls us to be content in Him regardless of our circumstances or marital status. Some times will prove to be more difficult than others. For me, it was during "break" times that my need for companionship was accentuated. During a two-week spring break in March, I needed to go through my library and catalog it. I thought of a sweet Christian girl who might be very helpful in this project. In fact, it seemed like a great idea!

Later, I was meditating on Matthew 4:1–11 and noted that Satan's first temptation was directed in the area of Jesus' obvious need. I felt that if I had fasted forty days and nights and someone suggested to me to turn stones into bread (and if I had the power to do so), I would genuinely thank them for the suggestion. Christ's response was different.

Christ recognized that He was being tempted to take matters into His own hands. He was being tempted to act independently of the Father. In the same way, on the surface there was nothing wrong with asking this Christian girl to aid me. However, God showed me that it was a "self-effort scheme" to meet my need for companionship. While it may not be wrong at all to place oneself in paths of legitimate conduct to meet people, a person does need to allow the Lord to search his heart. One's heart could either be at the extreme of fearfully avoiding the possibility of marriage or the other extreme of scheming to get needs met. In either case, what is not of faith is sin (Romans 14:22–23).

A dear friend and Christian businessman had shared with me the principle that on the other side of a temptation is often a special opportunity and provision of God. When Jim had started his own company, he found himself praying that God would give him a relationship with a certain businessman who had been quite successful in a similar venture. One day the phone rang, and it was this man. Jim's heart leaped for joy. He listened eagerly as he was being invited to accompany him and other men on a hunting and fishing trip in Mexico. Jim responded with delight but told the caller that he had two problems: "I don't hunt and I don't fish."

The successful businessman lowered his voice and told him, "We probably will not hunt or fish, but we plan to do some drinking and get some women." At that moment Jim had a choice to make. He so deeply desired the favor of this businessman, but God gave him the grace to say, "I have so desired to get to know you. I'd love to meet with you and play golf or another activity, but I am deeply in love with my wife and I would never do that."

Some time later this same businessman unexpectedly came into Jim's office. He told Jim, "I have some serious personal problems and thought that you might be the kind of person who could help me." God gave Jim a relationship with this man and the opportunity for ministry on the other side of the temptation. He received both as gifts from God and with a clean conscience!

The memory of God using Matthew 4 to reveal to me my temptation to scheme is vivid—not only because God gave me the grace to both recognize and resist the temptation to take matters into my own hands, but also because it was that very week that I met Penny. On the other side of the temptation was the provision of God. Proverbs 18:22 says, "He who finds a wife finds a good thing and obtains favor from the Lord." The Hebrew word for "find" does not denote a diligent search but rather finding something along one's normal and natural path of life.

4

REPENTING OF IDOLATRY AFTER EXPERIENCING LOVE AT FIRST SIGHT

MICHAEL WAS A DEAR FRIEND whom I met at church. He invited me to visit his place of ministry one day during my spring break. As I went to his office, I was "struck" as I noticed a certain young lady. Michael proceeded to take me on a long tour, but all I could think of was how I could get back to that office and talk to that young lady.

After the tour Michael took me to staff devotions where this same young lady was called on to pray. Her prayer seemed to reveal a tender heart toward God. Let me quickly say that first impressions can be very misleading and need to pass the test of time. While I was so struck by the impression that Penny had made on me that I missed my turn on my drive home, my impression on her was such that she does not even remember the day! However, her kindness and godly disposition arrested my attention.

ONE IMMEDIATE AND ONE "DELAYED" ANSWER TO PRAYER

After making it home to my apartment, I called my mother and asked her to pray with me that God would lead Penny's and my paths together again without me trying to make it happen. Less than a week later, I received an invitation to attend a surprise birthday party. As the person listed off who would be there, guess who was one of the people? I went to my journal and wrote an "A.P." to the right side of my request to note the "answer to prayer."

At this birthday party God gave me time with Penny before most of the guests arrived. This time seemed to confirm the impression that I sensed a week earlier during our first encounter. A sweet spirit was the dominant feature of her life. I was to leave the next day to fly back to Dallas to defend my dissertation and requested prayer from her.

When I flew back into Chicago, I desired to

call and thank the people who had prayed, as the Lord had greatly blessed the time in Dallas. I wanted to call Penny, but I did not know how to spell her last name. At church that Sunday, a small piece of paper fell from a friend's hand. I picked it up for him and noticed that it contained a list of names and phone numbers— including Penny's. Not even a sparrow or phone list falls to the ground apart from the Lord's control and direction! This short glance at the list informed me how to spell her last name. With this information I was able to secure her phone number and call her to thank her for her prayers.

I was the adviser to the junior class of Moody students that year, and the Junior-Senior Banquet was coming up in a few weeks. It is a semiformal occasion that allows for a fellow to escort a girl to it. As the advisor I was expected to go, and I sensed that Penny was the Lord's provision of whom I should ask. I called her again and asked her if she would like to go. She graciously accepted the invitation but also informed me of the arrangement that she had with her father—to approve any fellow who asked to spend time with her.

I was invited to her home for dinner and met her dad, and he gave his blessing to escort his daughter to the banquet. I hardly ever notice what a person wears, but I wrote in my journal,

"She looked incredibly sweet in a blue sweater, plaid skirt, and black shoes. Her heart for Scripture and sensitivity filled my thoughts, and it was a very pleasant thought (Philippians 4:8)!"

The night of the banquet came, and I drove up in my 1969 Camaro, which I had purchased thirteen years earlier. Having been in the South for virtually all of its life, it had no rust and I continually got offers from others to purchase it. A few months later I would accept one of those offers; however, this night it carried us to the banquet. And when one of the tailpipes fell off the following night, I praised God for the safe travel He had provided. There was not much else that happened that night that would have encouraged a fellow. Penny seemed to be looking forward to one thing—getting back home. As I drove her back to her home and later arrived at my apartment, I got down on my knees in front of my couch. I had noticed her special ability of making others feel comfortable. After meditating on Luke 11:1–13 on that night in April of 1982, I asked God to give Penny to me as my wife. On the following night in a phone conversation with her, she related to me that she had no peace to develop a relationship. It was clear that God had not answered that prayer yet! When I asked if it was all right to still call her, she said, "Sure."

The telephone calls became the extent of our relationship. About once a month I would call her, and we would talk about spiritual truths. On one occasion Penny did go with me to spend some time with a married couple who attended one of my classes at school, but later she again offered a reservation about our spending time together.

The spiritual battle in Penny's mind revolved around the question, *What is your way, Lord, of drawing two people together?* She had learned the importance of "guarding her heart" (see Proverbs 4:23) and keeping herself not only physically but also mentally and emotionally for one man. The spiritual battle in my mind was *What is wrong with me?* My mind would be tempted to imagine being somebody else that could instantly win her heart. My journal is full of entries of disappointment and even jealousy of others who seemed to enjoy more favor from her. It is also full of questions about whether my life could truly make a wife happy.

I praised God when I sensed freedom from Him to call and converse with her. We talked about our various spiritual disciplines and helpful spiritual input the Lord had given us. Our conversation revealed her heart for God. I would be tempted to think of other girls who I reasoned would be much more responsive to me, but God set Penny apart in my mind from all others. She had a radiant countenance that left me stunned.

God had clearly established the fact of my inadequacy to win her heart. I did petition Him to give it to me if it would honor His name and help me finish the work that He had for me (John 17:4). To keep my heart pure, I asked God to use me to increase her love and fear of Him and to make her even more beautiful and radiant for Christ.

The telephone calls continued until, following one phone conversation, I experienced great discouragement in my soul after I hung up the phone. Talking to myself I inquired, "Why are you so down?" I discovered that it was clearly because of Penny's apparent lack of response to me. Pondering why her response had such an impact upon me, I came to the realization that she had become an idol in my life. An idol is someone or something that one looks to meet the thirsts of the heart. There was nothing wrong with Penny, but I needed to get my heart right with God.

The Lord drew my attention to 1 Corinthians 10:14, which contains the command to "flee from idolatry." All I was doing was calling her on the phone, but in obedience to this verse, I ceased the calls. For a period of a year I had no correspondence with her in any way.

5

REBIRTH OF THE VISION: PURIFY MY HEART AMIDST CLOSED DOORS

ONE NIGHT I received a long-distance call from Michael Pearson in Portland, Oregon. He is the dear friend I had visited in March of 1982 and during this occasion had first met Penny. He called to see how I was doing and inquire about my relationship with her. I related to him the story I have just written about how God had dealt with the idolatry in my heart and that I had not had any correspondence with her in the past year. Michael communicated to me that he had talked to Penny the previous evening and asked her about me. He informed me that she thought highly of me. This was news to me. He

strongly encouraged me to pursue a relationship with her. He did let me know that there was
another fellow in her life but said, "Don't worry
about it."

As I hung up the phone that night, I felt very
loved because of Mike's expression of concern
for me. I sought God during the next month,
asking Him to let me know if it was truly Him
encouraging me to take the initiative in this relationship. One day I felt the freedom to write a
letter to her while I was studying in a library with
a colleague. Mike's call had been God's means
of once again establishing communication.

I learned later the circumstances in which
Penny received this letter. She had just finished
reading through the Bible for that year and was
praying on the front steps of her house. She expressed these words to God, "I do not want
what is good or even what may be better, but,
God, give me Your absolute *best* in all areas of
my life." At that moment the mailman arrived
with my letter. The last line of the letter read,
"May God give you His *best* in all ways and at
all times."

After the month of prayer I felt a freedom to
once again call Penny, and we experienced the
best conversations that had ever occurred in our
relationship. I marveled at how God had seem-
ingly encouraged me to once again get into the

relationship after laying it down in response to His loving rebuke from 1 Corinthians 10:14.

THE CHALLENGE
TO PURIFY MY HEART

In the midst of numerous delightful conversations, I learned that Penny's relationship with the other fellow was growing. This knowledge came just as I was about to take the step of initiating spending time together with her. I strongly sensed that it would not be appropriate to do so at this time. I called and told her that I would not be calling anymore, but I did truly wish her the best in every way. God had put on my heart the conviction to encourage her to throw her life behind the other fellow, because this kind of support is what truly brings the best out of a man! I could not say this with my emotions, but in my will I said it out of obedience to God. In my emotions, I desired her to throw her life in another direction! I even offered to meet with them if I could ever be of encouragement.

After I finished the phone call I attempted to go to bed. My heart beat fast all night, and I did not sleep at all. I realized how much my heart had been attached to this relationship. It was a relief to know that it was over. God comforted me the next day through a conversation with my mother.

A NEW BEGINNING AND ANOTHER CLOSED DOOR

In May 1987 (the first meeting was in March of 1982) I sensed a strong prompting to give Penny a call on a graduation day at school. As I talked to her I sensed that her spirit was down. When I learned that the other relationship had not worked out, my spirit was up! The telephone calls began again, and on one summer day we took a walk together. In the fall on another occasion, I taught a Bible study in the home of her parents. In December 1987 and January 1988 we spent quite a bit of time together in her home. Penny and three of her friends enrolled in an evening class I was to teach on Thursday nights.

On the Monday following Valentine's Day, Penny's father gave me a call at work. He arranged a time when we could get together the next day for lunch. I met Dr. Bauer and we went down the street to a nice Chinese restaurant in downtown Chicago.

Over lunch he related to me how the family had met last night and talked about me. He stated how they admired my character qualities and the kind of person I was. However, for a reason that Penny could not fully explain, she could not envision me as being her mate.

As I excused myself to the men's room, my emotions overtook me and I burst into tears. The relationship had known numerous closed doors, or, as some term it, "deaths to a vision," but this seemed the most final. I had thought it was over before, but this time I knew it. I told Dr. Bauer that I would deeply miss the fellowship with his family. Afterward, we walked back to my office and had a special time of prayer together. We prayed that God would bless my relationships with all the people that I had met through her and all of Penny's relationships with the people that she had met through me. There was a joy in the pain, and this experience knit my heart to Penny's father in a special way.

6

EXPERIENCING GOD'S PROVIDENCE AND DELAYED ANSWERS TO PRAYERS

THE ONLY CONTACT I had with Penny at this period was on Thursday nights when she and three of her friends would attend my evening class on the Corinthian Epistles. Unknown to me until over a year later was that when Penny walked into the first night of class, two female students said to each other, "That's the girl for Dr. Thrasher. Let's pray about it."

I had lived without a car in Chicago ever since I had sold my 1969 Camaro. Spending all of my life's savings, I had purchased it new and kept it for fourteen years. When I arrived in Chicago from the sunny South, it was rust free and looked new even though it was eleven years old. Like I said, I often received notes inquiring if I would sell it. I was happy to sell it and received only four hundred dollars less than I had paid for it new. As I considered getting another car to replace it, I pondered whether or not I really needed one. I lived right across from the commuter train to Chicago and was also within walking distance to most of the places that I frequented in Wheaton. As a single person I could have easily lived without a car. I learned later that it was a concern to Penny that I did not have a car. She thought, *Can he afford a car? Can he afford a wife?* She is grateful now because I saved all the car expenses and put them into a fund that later enabled us to buy a house.

As I began to speak in churches more often, a car became more of a necessity. The almost six years without a car had been freeing and enabled me to save a lot of money, but the purchase of a 1988 Honda Prelude was helpful in making the most of the ministry doors God was opening. Penny was still the one I wanted to share my joys with. After calling Penny to let her know of God's provision, her mother encouraged her to call me and invite me to have supper with the family to celebrate the purchase.

That evening in her home I felt totally free in the relationship for the first time. I remembered Ben Haden, a pastor in Chattanooga, Tennessee, asking me one key question before he hired me for a pastoral internship. "Has God ever broken your heart?" he inquired. "That is a key preparation for ministry, because you will be ministering to people who have broken hearts," he continued. I did not know how to answer him then, but I knew this night that God had used this relationship to break my heart. However, He had done it in the most merciful way possible, for I knew it had been broken in the context of still knowing the acceptance of her family. As we took a walk that evening, I told her of God's tender mercies in breaking my heart.

On Sundays during this time, I often attended a 7:00 A.M. Bible study that Penny and her family also attended. This particular Sunday morning she was the only member of her family who attended. At the conclusion of the study, the group would have a session of prayer and then go to their respective churches. During the time of prayer, Penny became so dizzy that she could hardly stand up and needed someone to drive her home. In God's providence I was the only one available to do so. After taking her home, I drove her dad back to the home of the Bible study, and he was able to drive Penny's car back to their home.

Although I had planned to return to my

church for Sunday service, I stayed with the Bauers and had lunch with them. I asked permission to talk to Penny, who was recuperating in her room from the sickness that would last about three days. During this time in her room she asked me, "At the end of your life, what would you like to have accomplished for God's glory?" I later learned that my reply was almost the identical words that she had written down the previous day. As I left her home, I sensed I would never see her again.

A DELAYED ANSWER TO PRAYER

On a Wednesday evening in June of 1988, I was shocked to receive a phone call from Penny. What I did not know was that the Lord had spoken to her heart during those three days of sickness. He had used the Word of God, the witness of the Spirit, providential circumstances, and the counsel of her parents. On the phone that night she shared with me that God had given her the freedom to deepen our friendship.

The call was a great encouragement. I communicated to her how much I appreciated it, but my heart was "numb" and I really did not know how to respond. After sharing some concerns with her that I learned later left her greatly discouraged, the phone call ended.

We all know how important it is to be able to rest in another's love and not feel like you have to perform for it. If He desires you to marry someone, He will give you this person's heart. What I did not realize was that God had done this at this point.

I called ten people in the next day that knew me and loved me and asked them to pray for direction. The days ahead were filled with events and happenings that I knew were an answer to these people's prayers. No matter who you are and how much you seek God, this area of our life is too big for any one of us to handle. We need the prayers, counsel, and support of others!

Penny and her family were going on a two-week vacation to a cottage on Lake Michigan. She invited me to go with them. I was able to go the first week and then returned to Chicago the following week to teach a one-week class to pastors and missionaries. After returning from the vacation, I met with Dr. B. Wayne Hopkins to prepare for our week of teaching together.

As we prepared for the class, I told him that I desired him to know what was going on in my life and related to him the latest development in my relationship with Penny. I figured he would have some "red flag," and that would be the end of it. He patiently listened, and as we were driving to downtown Chicago the following day, he asked me, "When are you going to ask her to marry you?"

The week of teaching was a wonderful one as I taught all day and lived downtown for that week in an apartment on campus. However, on Wednesday night I could not sleep. As I tossed and turned in bed, a strange thing came to mind. I recalled a prayer that I had prayed over sixteen years ago.

As a college student at Auburn University in 1972, I was reading Luke 6:12. The thought of Jesus staying up all night to pray before He chose His disciples struck me. As I pondered this verse, I thought, *A disciple is someone you influence. Who would I influence? I guess a wife is whom I would influence for better or worse if it is God's will for me to marry. I pray that I would be able to stay up all night and pray before I propose.* I prayed this naïve prayer very seriously in 1972, but I had never thought about it again until this night.

It was not because I was so godly that I had decided to stay up all night. It was that I could not sleep, and the Lord brought back this prayer of sixteen years ago to my mind and was in the midst of answering it. I had completely forgotten the prayer, but God had carefully stored it up at His throne of grace and answered it in His perfect timing and way. I did stay up all night and attempted to pray with some anticipation. Normally I would have been concerned about the strength to teach the following day from 8:00 A.M. to 5:00 P.M. It was not a concern, and the Lord gave me strength for the next day.

The following night, I was obviously exhausted as I hopped into bed. Tomorrow would be Friday, and I only had to teach half a day. I would then drive six hours north to Michigan and spend the weekend with Penny and her family. Immediately I sensed a need to get out of bed and go to my office and call my mother (my father was no longer living). I told her that I would be traveling to Michigan to see Penny for the final weekend of her family's vacation. I asked her, "What is your counsel for me in this relationship? I need to know if you have any concerns."

She told me, "I don't think you have ever felt toward anyone like you do for Penny. You have my total blessing. Do what you think is best."

After I arrived in Frankfurt, Michigan, on Friday night I took a walk with Penny and told her that we needed to clarify our relationship. She immediately responded, "Yes, we do." I had never encountered that type of response before.

As I went to sleep in my little room of the family cottage, I thought about what I had said: "We need to clarify our relationship." There was obviously no way to do this without talking about marriage. I knew that I needed to talk to her father and obtain permission to do so. Before going to sleep, I prayed that I would be the first one up in the cottage the next morning and that her dad would be the second. That is exactly how it happened.

I asked Dr. Bauer for permission to sit down and talk with him. We went outside close to the beach, and I shared with him my conversation with Penny last night. I told him that I did not know how to clarify our relationship without talking about marriage, and I desired to ask his permission to do so. To this he replied, "Marriage is all there is left to talk about." I did not realize that God had opened their hearts in this way. Her dad and I prayed, committing the relationship into the Lord's hands and prayed for His guidance for the most meaningful way to propose.

In order to appreciate this next little confirmation, I will need to take you back to a conversation between Penny and her dad a few years previously. She earnestly desired God's confirmation in this area of her life and had been influenced by a statement by Dr. Charles Stanley's grandfather. He had said that God will move heaven and earth to make clear His will. She told her father, "This is what I want. I want

God to send a shooting star, as a message in the sky, to let me know His will." Her dad replied with a grin, "Yes, you probably want the shooting star in the daytime!"

On July 16, 1988, I took Penny for a walk along the beach of Lake Michigan and that night read her portions of my journal about how God had led me to this occasion. I related how over six years ago I had asked God to give me her as a wife after the banquet in April of 1982. I asked her to marry me and she said, "Yes!" She looked up and exclaimed, "Look, there is a shooting star!" There really was! She said "yes" first, and God's "rejoicing" star in response was both special and humorous.

Permit me to close my part of the story with a prayer that all of us can join together and pray for each other and ourselves:

> Thank You, Lord, for these readers and Your love for them and Your knowledge of their deepest desires and aspirations. Build a wall of protection around them to protect them from the wrong people, and mold them into the beautiful people You designed them to be. In Your timing and will, lead them into marriages that are clearly of You. On their wedding days, may there only be tears of joy—not tears of regret and sorrow. May You do something in each

of our lives that could bring great rejoicing in heaven for all eternity. At each of our vulnerable moments, send Your heavenly support in our lives. Give us the grace to believe You for Your best, and may You never forget this prayer, but remember it day and night and act upon it as each day requires.

May the following chapters be used of You to answer this prayer. For Your glory and our eternal benefit. Amen.

A FEW LESSONS IN RETROSPECT

1. All of us need a preparation time of single-ness before marriage.

2. Certain times may be harder than others in trusting God with your singleness. These times can be ones of intense temptation.

3. On the other side of a temptation often is a special opportunity and provision of God.

4. You do not need to try to be somebody you are not in order to win the heart of the other person you admire.

5. God will draw two people together in His sovereignty if He wills them to be married.

6. Do not let another be an idol in your life. An "idol" is someone or something that you look to in order to fulfill the thirsts of your heart to feel important and secure.

7. What is of God might go through various "deaths of a vision" before it is fulfilled.

8. We need the support, counsel, and prayers of others in this area of our lives no matter how much we might be seeking God.

9. Seek to honor both sets of parents.

10. Making the most of one's singleness is the best preparation for marriage.

11. Live today in a way that will do your future mate good.

12. Thoughtfully present your sexual energies and drives to God, and vow to keep yourselves pure for one man or one woman.

LEARNING FROM THE OTHER SIDE OF THE STORY

PENNY'S STORY

"WOULD YOU GRANT ME a life message in the area of courtship?" was my heart's cry to the Lord as a woman in my midtwenties. What is a life message? It is a personal story that reveals who God is—leading to praise, worship, trust, and faith-filled action. In asking for this life message, I had no idea the whirlwind the Lord would take me through, but in it He revealed His precious self.

I grew up in a loving Christian home—the last of four children. At age five I asked Jesus to save me and let me live with Him forever in heaven when I die. Through the years He has nurtured our relationship through His Word, using my godly parents and those of their generation to mentor me. I never dated in high school or in college. It wasn't until after college while working in a Christian ministry with God-seeking, dynamic singles that my heart awakened to the hope of marriage.

The unwritten code among us was "attention toward all, intention toward none." I was exhorted to "guard my heart with all diligence, for from it flows the springs of life" (see Proverbs 4:23). Consequently, we singles fellowshipped in groups, not pairing off. The Lord gave us marvelous times, and we had great freedom to exhort one another to love and good deeds and to serve the Lord together with our strength, devotion, and enthusiasm. In the inner recesses of my heart, I was yearning to do my husband good all the days of my life (Proverbs 31:12), even before I knew who he was. This transformed me into pursuing the Lord with all my heart while keeping myself for one man only.

My father is a wonderful, godly man. He traveled a lot during my younger years. When I was older, I deeply desired a stronger relationship with him and needed his counsel. One day while driving along with him in the car, I asked him what his vision for me was. Without a moment's hesitation he responded, "To be a wife and a mother."

To be a wife and a mother! I thought exasperatingly. *I can't do a thing about either!* I felt as if I were in limbo. Yes, I desired marriage, but as I approached thirty, I was not at all sure God had that for me. Should I pursue a ministry, further study, or missions with all thoughts of marriage aside? How could I just "wait around" for the right one? What was my purpose in life now?

In my job, one of my responsibilities was to read the president's mail, and, with guidance, answer it. Many of the letters came from disgruntled women lamenting their marriages. Fear began rising in my heart. Some of these women truly believed it was God's will when they got married. Can we be so deceived as to miss God's best? I began seriously doubting my ability to make the right choice. "O Father," I prayed, "if you have marriage for me, let me know that the one I end up marrying is Your choice!" I knew that whatever difficulties would arise in my marriage, I could have greater strength knowing I had obeyed His leading. The question that naturally followed was, "Lord, what is Your design in bringing two people together?"

Laura, a godly coworker and dear friend, and I were searching the Scriptures, especially the

Old Testament for answers. We saw the Lord bringing two people together (like Adam and Eve) or using the parents to arrange marriages (like Isaac and Rebecca). The case we noted in Judges 14 when Samson married a woman because "she looked good to him," going against his parents' counsel, ended in disaster!

How I wanted a Psalm 1 man whose delight and daily meditation was in the law of the Lord —a Psalm 15 man who walked in integrity! A Psalm 112 man is one who fears the Lord and greatly delights in His commandments. I wrote in the margin of my Bible by that psalm, "Oh, Father, may my husband be such a man! And may I be such a woman."

Was I being realistic? Were my sights set too high? As different young men expressed interest in me (of which my husband was one) I asked a godly older woman how I could know God's will. She replied, "God will show His will to those who really want it."

"With all my heart I want to know Your perfect will and have the grace to do it," I pleaded. It was at this time that I was getting to know a young engineer and his sister. My brother and I would do various activities with the two of them. It was amazing what we had in common. Our siblings' personalities were incredibly similar. Our fathers were German—German engineers who owned their own companies. Their firms were right across the street from one another in downtown Chicago.

This young man was aspiring to be the president of his father's firm one day. I knew family business—what it was like to pray for a contract, go through the bidding process, the disappointments, the lean times as well as those of abundance. I knew what it was like to have the head of the home travel worldwide. Could this be God's choice for me?

We memorized Scripture together, reached out to the needy, and pursued each other's interests with delight. We traveled many miles in a red Honda Prelude. In the beginning of our getting to know one another, we made the commitment that if at any time our families were not for our relationship, we would stop seeing each other.

Everything was a green light. We were headed toward an engagement, waiting for the appropriate timing. My prayer had become the prayer of Moses in Exodus when he asked the Lord not to lead him up from there (the wilderness) unless His presence (favor and blessing) went with him. This young man's father, who was often the hardest to please, accepted me graciously. But we started to notice a resistance in his mother toward me. It became more and more evident as time went on. To honor her, we stopped seeing each other. God was asking me, like Abraham of the Old Testament, to yield up my "Isaac." God gave me the grace to do it; but, with travail of soul, I asked Him for "a three-day Moriah." (Abraham labored under the burden of having to sacrifice Isaac for three days since it took him that long to journey to Mount Moriah where he was to build the altar.) At the end of three days this man's mother called me and said, "You and my son have been like Abraham and Isaac. Who am I to stand in the way?" Needless to say, our joy knew a new level.

But it wasn't to last. About two months later, his mother's heart again turned away from me—a situation that couldn't be explained by the daughters. None could understand. We again honored her by not seeing or talking to one another. It was over.

With the end of that relationship went the death of a deep heart's desire—to minister to pastors and missionaries by providing them with retreats to come away and be refreshed. My heart would not heal. I felt as if I was in open-heart surgery for four months. It wasn't until we released each other from commitments we had made that I began to heal. Isaiah 50:10–51:3 became dear to me.

My husband to be, Bill, walked back into my

life. He had been and continued to be the most godly young man I knew. Our telephone conversations centered on Scripture and godly thinking and living. In many ways, he discipled me by his love for the Lord and his life's expression of that love. As he spent time in my parents' home and led Bible studies, we all began to highly value his friendship. There were other young godly men who were in my life. How was I to know God's choice?! I thought I knew before, but God clearly had shut that door!

Charles Stanley is a wonderful preacher in Georgia. His grandfather had received special intervention from the Lord and believed God could move heaven and earth to show him His perfect will. I expressed my desire to my father, "I wish God would write my future husband's name in the sky with His stars!" He responded, "Yes. You would want it in the daytime!"

I was having a difficult time envisioning Bill as my husband. Yet I couldn't get him off my heart. God got my attention when I asked Bill what he would like to have accomplished for the Lord at the end of his life and his response matched mine. I fasted and prayed. God led me through His Word.

Was Bill a Psalm 1 and Psalm 112 man? My heart said a resounding, *Yes!* He was then in the middle of his twenty-year goal of meditating on every verse of the Bible. Was he a man of integrity? Oh, yes. And the testimony of others who knew him confirmed this. Then the Holy Spirit led me to Hosea 2:19 in which the Lord says, "I will betroth you to Me forever; yes, I will betroth you to Me in righteousness and in justice, in lovingkindness and in compassion, and I will betroth you to Me in faithfulness. Then you will know the Lord."

Bill had been so Christlike in our relationship. He was righteous and just. He had been so loving in telling me to throw my life behind that other fellow, and then Bill had withdrawn his pursuit of me. He had been very compassionate, not only to me but to others as well. And above all, he had been faithful over six long years! I felt an incredible peace I had not known before toward anyone.

I called a family meeting, explaining what the Lord had shown me in Scripture. "What do you think, Daddy?" He confirmed my thoughts. I turned to my mother, "And you? Do you envision Bill as my husband?"

"I always have," was her response.

"What do I do now?" I asked.

My dad replied, "You tell him what you have told us. If he calls in the next day or so, tell him. If he does not call, you call him." Bill did not call.

With trembling hands I called him. I felt if I told him all that God had shown me, I would, in fact, be proposing to him. I didn't want that; nor did I know where his heart was now. All I could think of saying was, "God has given me a new freedom to deepen our friendship." Bill, of course, did not know how to interpret that statement—hence, his calling ten friends to ask for prayer.

After it all came together—his being with us at our cottage in Michigan, sharing his diary with my father and later with me, his proposal to me on my favorite beach on Lake Michigan that had become my "prayer closet," and my enthusiastic "Yes!"—I lifted my eyes to the heavens to see a shooting star. It was God's personal sign of rejoicing with us; my wonderful heavenly Father had given me the desire of my heart. He had given me a marriage arranged by Him, confirmed by Him, and ordained by Him! He had given me more than my heart's desires; He resurrected my vision of serving pastors and missionaries. Bill not only ministers to pastors and missionaries, he is one! And Bill is *my* ministry! What a magnificent, personal God and loving Abba Father.

DEVELOPING
A CONVICTION
BEFORE GOD

ABOUT TWO YEARS after I (Bill) read the book *Silhouettes: Women Behind Great Men*, which I referred to in chapter 2, God opened a door to go to Chicago and join the faculty at the Moody Bible Institute. The school flew me up for a "house-hunting trip." They offered to rent me a car to aid me in the exploration of a place to live. I told them that this was not necessary because I would be content to live on campus. They replied, "We do not have anywhere for faculty members to live on campus at this time."

I told them that was fine, but I would like to live "close" because my life in these early years would be my teaching and finishing my dissertation. The director of personnel answered, "I commute sixty miles one way. Close is a relative term in Chicago." I knew we were using the same word but evidently a different dictionary. I grew up in the South, and "close" to me meant walking to work.

I declined the gracious offer of the car and went down the street to explore an apartment to rent. To this day I do not remember where I went, but I do remember the shocking price. At that point, I decided to take the train out to the suburbs. I pulled out a map of Chicago and decided to take the train to Wheaton, simply because it was the only suburb with which I was familiar. A gracious real estate lady took me around even though she knew that I would only rent and that she would receive no commission. After looking at a number of places, we discussed a high-rise apartment right across from the train. This was a wonderful provision as I could catch the train each morning with the convenience of a two-minute walk.

The amazing thing is that after I set up my residence on the second floor of this twenty-story high-rise apartment, I learned that Stephen and Heather Olford, whom I spoke about in chapter 2, lived in the same building on the nineteenth floor! After making their acquaintance we became friends. Each time I would see Mrs. Olford, I would renew my conviction not to "seek a wife" but to wait on God's provision.

Waiting is a very important aspect of the Christian life, but it is not easy. It is difficult to wait on God for His provision of a life partner. The gift of perspective is something that God offers to you free of charge, but it was at great expense to Him. The gift of being controlled by His love and delivered from living only for ourselves was purchased by Christ's sacrificial and substitutionary death.

> *For the love of Christ controls us, having concluded this, that one died for all, therefore all died; and He died for all, so that they who live might no longer live for themselves, but for Him who died and rose again on their behalf.* (2 Corinthians 5:14–15)

It is not wrong to desire marriage, for God created us with needs that He often uses marriage to fulfill. Only as we are able to put these desires in perspective are we able to trust Him with these desires. If we think only of ourselves, it is impossible to trust God in this area. However, if we delight in the Lord who has delivered us from living only for ourselves, the question is now, "How do You desire me to use my singleness as I wait on You for Your will and provision of a marriage partner?"[1]

God may be giving you a great opportunity to build His truth into your life. Also, it is easier to continue one's studies while single. This freedom was very helpful to me in my long years of education. For you as well, the freedom to spend your evenings studying and serving gives you an availability to the Lord and others that is not possible when you are married. This does not take the desire for marriage away, but it does allow you to put it in perspective.

Many of us can relate to feeling alone when we are at a couple-dominated gathering and are without a companion or life partner. I remember the testimony of a very godly single lady who had ministered around the world. She talked about this lonely feeling she experienced each time she attended a wedding ceremony. Through continuous prayer, she learned to give that time at the wedding to the Lord and look to Him to deliver her from the temptation to feel sorry for herself.

It is a mouthful to say that we need to let God *train* us to look to Him alone for our ultimate sense of security and significance. Only in this way will our ultimate sense of well-being not be determined by the presence or absence of a mate. Isn't a key theme of godly singleness contentment?

THE MEANING OF CONTENTMENT

Not that I speak from want, for I have learned to be content in whatever circumstances I am. I know how to get along with humble means, and I also know how to live in prosperity; in any and every circumstance I have learned the secret of being filled and going hungry, both of having abundance and suffering need. I can do all things through Him who strengthens me. (Philippians 4:11–13)

According to this passage, contentment is not something that is innate to us. It has to be learned. It is also something that can be experienced in any circumstance.

For this reason, Jeremiah Burroughs, in his work entitled *The Rare Jewel of Christian Contentment*, defines contentment as a "sweet, inward, gracious form of Spirit which freely submits to and delights in God's wise and fatherly disposal in every condition."[2]

There is a great freedom in contentment. It is freedom from the stress of our self-effort attempts to "get ahead" and accomplish "our" agendas. There is a freedom from being controlled by the desire for status and possessions.

Those desires spring from selfish ambition, which is at the root of the wisdom of the world (James 3:14–15).

Contentment gives one the freedom to rejoice in God's gracious provision in the present moment. In the next chapter we will learn the secret of contentment.

9

DISCOVERING
THE SECRET OF
CONTENTMENT

PAUL NOT ONLY SAID that he had learned the secret of contentment Philippians 4:12, but he also openly shares it in the next verse. The secret is to realize that all one needs is in Jesus and what He chooses to provide. This is what the psalmist declares after his great struggles with discontentment and jealousy, "Whom have I in heaven but You? And besides You, I desire nothing on earth" (Psalm 73:25).

One must trust God to rebuild his or her thought structures concerning the person of God. When Paul penned these words in Philippians 4, he was not in a palace but in a prison.

However, he did not only see himself in prison but also in Christ. Look at the amazing words of 1 Corinthians 3:21–23:

> *So then let no one boast in men. For all things belong to you, whether Paul or Apollos or Cephas or the world or life or death or things present or things to come; all things belong to you, and you belong to Christ; and Christ belongs to God.*

Observe the phrase "all things belong to you." I spent a year asking God what these words meant. I came to the conclusion that they show the adequacy of God for us in every situation. All you or I will ever need to fulfill His will for our lives He will provide and not one minute later than we need it. Any help from another person, or any provision from the world, any blessing in life or death, any present or future blessing—all of this belongs to Him. These blessings have been given to us in order to serve our wonderful Savior and Master, Jesus Christ, because we belong to Him. We have earned His judgment, but in His grace all things belong to us in Christ.

Trust is the key to contentment. We must realize that God is always in control and that He is good. If this were not true, He could never give His children the promise of Romans 8:28:

And we know that God causes all things to work together for good to those who love God, to those who are called according to His purpose.

He is absolutely faithful to provide all we need to fulfill His will, which is exactly what we would desire if we knew all the facts. Helen Keller, who was blind and unable to hear, spoke of so enjoying what God had given her that she had no time to think about what she did not have. When we long for another person, position, or possession, we are experiencing the same emotion that God has toward us at that moment. He is always thinking of His people:

> *Many, O Lord my God,*
> *are the wonders which You have done,*
> *And Your thoughts toward us;*
> *There is none to compare with You.*
> *If I would declare and speak of them,*
> *They would be too numerous to count.*
>
> (Psalm 40:5)

HOW TO EXPERIENCE CONTENTMENT

In order to experience contentment, we must learn to delight in the Lord and repent of anything that is hindering a flourishing relationship with God. A verse that may seem far away and inapplicable from us is Isaiah 48:22, which states, "There is no peace for the wicked."

You say, "Yes, that is right; they do not deserve peace and contentment." But let me ask you one question, "What is more wicked than telling God that He cannot rule over an area of your life?" To do so is to spurn His great gift of peace and contentment. In the testimony of my own courtship, I related how God convicted me of idolatry. In this case I sensed that God was directing me to end my relationship. In this case it was also resurrected some years later.

What do you do when you long for another person? Remember that it is not a sin to be tempted (Hebrews 4:15). First of all, you can thank God for your normal desire. It is natural to long for companionship and intimacy. In order to not let this longing take your thoughts in the wrong direction, bring your thoughts in the light to God and share them with Him. Reaffirm the truth of His knowledge of your needs and desires and of His loving care for you. Be honest in your conversation with Him. Trust Him to fulfill your desires in His righteous ways and perfect timing (John 7:37–39). In order not to unduly live in the future, ask Him also to make the most of your singleness for His glory. As Jim Elliot said, "Wherever you are, be all there."[1]

THE FRUITFULNESS OF CONTENTMENT

How does God desire to use you as you wait on Him for His person, timing, and will in marriage? Does He desire you to be an integral part of reviving His church? Do you long to see His manifested presence among His people, actively at work convicting the lost and drawing men and women to Himself as well as guiding and directing His people? Ask God to use you to be a vessel to restore His church to experience His presence. God's loving discipline often takes the form of Him withdrawing His manifested presence in the same way that His glory departed from the temple in the Old Testament. To be sure, the Holy Spirit who indwells every Christian will never leave, but His presence can be grieved and quenched and, therefore, God's name is not adored and honored as it should be. How does God desire to use you? We all have different roles, but each of us is an important and vital part of God's overall plan.

A single person is not only freer to pursue his or her vocation but also to develop friendships. The physical and emotional energy that would be expended in marriage can be channeled into relationships with other single people, married couples and families, and even children. All have a need to love and be loved, and God is able to meet this need even in our "dark moments."

As you respond to the Lord in your single years, you are not only giving yourself the best preparation for marriage but also building a spiritual heritage for future generations. Fanny Crosby was given a wrong medical treatment at six weeks of age that resulted in permanent blindness. As a child she made up her mind to store in her heart what she called the "little jewel of contentment." She declared this jewel to be the "comfort of her life." When she was eight years old she wrote:

> O what a happy soul am I!
> Although I cannot see,
> I am resolved that in this world
> Contented I will be.
>
> How many blessings I enjoy
> that other people don't.
> To weep and sigh because I'm blind;
> I cannot, and I won't.

Scores of people have been blessed through the legacy of hymns she has left the church, and millions have been blessed by her learning the lesson of contentment in God's sovereign will.

Fanny Crosby married Alexander Van Alstyne

when she was thirty-eight. This dear couple experienced a great loss when their only child died at a very young age. In her grief she penned the hymn "Safe in the Arms of Jesus." A ministry borne out of a humble and contented heart bears great fruit.

A carriage driver discovered her as his passenger one day and told her as he wept how they had sung "Safe in the Arms of Jesus" at his little girl's funeral the previous week. Even more amazing is the testimony of seven prisoners of war who were singled out to be killed by firing squad. As the day of their death arrived, one of the prisoners began to sing "Safe in the Arms of Jesus," a song he had learned three weeks earlier. As he sung, one of the other prisoners dropped to his knees and began to pray. Then all seven began to sing! The officer was so impressed with the prisoners' contentment and courage as they faced death that he trusted Christ as his Savior that very hour. Only God can tell what comes from a life that allows Him to put His contentment inside the soul.

MAKING AN
IMPORTANT
COMMITMENT

A NUMBER OF YEARS AGO I received a letter from Ted, who is a faithful missionary in Mexico, requesting prayer for the Christian young people in the church who were struggling with the idea of waiting on the Lord for a believing life partner. The temptation to settle for an unbeliever or a life of impurity is very intense. He wrote of two in his fellowship who had stopped following Christ over this very issue. Often, older singles struggle as they wonder if they will ever marry.

A girl can be tempted to play at sex in order to try and secure love. In fact, even flirting may

be read as an advertisement that one is inter-
ested in an improper physical relationship. Im-
modest clothing—tight-fitting, see-through, or
low-cut items—may be read in the same way,
even though it often stems from the desire to be
noticed and genuinely loved. Such defrauding
action can arouse appetites that cannot be
righteously fulfilled and invite devastating consequences into a person's life.

On the other hand, a guy might pretend to
be loving and caring in order to secure a sinful
physical relationship. Such lines as, "If you
really loved me you would . . ."; "Don't be old-
fashioned . . ."; "You won't get pregnant"; and
"I get so excited with you that I just can't stop"
are reflections of mishandling of the heart and
mind of a girl. This can lead to countless future
problems in both of their lives.

God created us to live in liberty. Liberty is
not the freedom to live as you desire but to live
as you ought to. How can we experience this
freedom in our sex lives? The best way to make
a right choice in the midst of these pressures is
to make it before you enter a relationship. A
vow is a very serious thing. The motivation for
a vow is not to try to atone for past guilt. However, there are occasions you deeply desire to experience something that you clearly know is
God's will. In regard to this, you can make a

commitment that you desire to be held accountable. The comfort of such a scriptural vow is that
God will send the support of heaven to help you
fulfill it!

One of the most important commitments
that any man can make is to be a one-woman
man and for a woman to be a one-man woman.
Such is the description in Scripture of a godly
man (1 Timothy 3:2) and a godly woman (1 Timothy 2:9). Such a vow involves specifically dedi-
cating your sexual drives and energies to God
for Him to fulfill in His perfect timing and righteous way. If God has marriage for you, this
opens you up to the enablement of God to re-
main pure in your thoughts and actions for the
person you will one day marry. In this sense one
can understand the description of the godly
woman in Proverbs 31:12 who does her husband good *all* the days of her life. This commitment enables her to do her spouse good
even before she knows who he is! And a man
can do the same thing for his future wife.

Author David Seamonds encourages young
people to write letters to their future spouses
even before they know them. It can be given to
your spouse on your wedding night. You might
describe how God has preserved you and directed
you to him or her to be the man or the woman
in your life. Such a commitment enables one to

overcome powerful temptation that can bring regretful thoughts like, *I never would have done this in high school or college if only I had known that I would eventually meet a person like* _____.

Seamonds continues by relating a fascinating story about a letter that a young pastor friend of his received. Of his friend in his late twenties, Seamonds wrote:

> On one such occasion he was conducting a special series of meetings for a church in a distant city. He had been staying in the spacious home of a wealthy church family. Late one night he was awakened by Jackie, the beautiful eighteen-year-old daughter of the family. She said she had fallen in love with him and wanted to have sex with him. Gently but firmly, he talked her out of it. She returned to her own bedroom embarrassed and in tears. Seven years later he received a note, the kind one receives from a bride in appreciation for a wedding present. Puzzled, he checked with his wife, who confirmed that no gift had been sent. They thought it was a mistake until another tiny note fell out of this fold. It was from Jackie, warmly thanking him for giving her the most valuable wedding gift she had received— her virginity![1]

God takes care of what you present to Him. When you present your sexual energies and drives to God, He is able to channel this energy into useful and productive service until marriage. I remember many years ago Stephen Olford saying, "If you yield your mind to Jesus Christ, you will be an intelligent Christian. If you yield your heart to Christ, you will be a devotional Christian. If you yield your will to Christ, you will be a forceful Christian. But if you yield your sex life to Christ, you will be a dynamic Christian." He related this truth to the Holy Spirit reigning in and flowing out of our innermost being (John 7:37–39).

God is not trying to simply restrain people but rather guide them into fruitful and fulfilling lives. Roger Staubach, the famous quarterback for the Dallas Cowboys, was once asked in an interview how he compared himself to another famous quarterback who had a reputation of being sexually active with multiple women. He replied, "I am just as sexually active, but all of my activity is with my beloved wife." God's ways do not limit you but rather guide you into the best, safest, and most fulfilling path of life.

Both a man and a woman desire to be loved unconditionally. This is far different than I love you *if* you go out with me, *if* you sleep with me, etc. It is far different than I love you *because* you are attractive, *because* you are athletic, etc. Everyone yearns to be loved in a way that he is free to share his weaknesses and not risk losing another's love.

It is for this reason that God's plan is to have the physical relationship of sex experienced with secure, unconditional love in the context of a permanent and mutual commitment of marriage. Love is the key to sex, but sex is not the key to love. In fact, one person after having intercourse may be saying, "I love you," and the other person may be saying, "I love it." The gentleness and kindness of God is behind His commands to abstain from sexual immorality (1 Corinthians 6:18; 1 Thessalonians 4:3).

Elisabeth Elliot, the noted missionary stateswoman, received the following letter from a woman who begged her to pass her story on:

> At seventeen years of age I chose to rebel against God and entered a relationship with my boyfriend that delivered not happiness but guilt and grief. I "fell in love" and rather than trust God, I went after the object of my desire with all the wiles and passions of a teenage romantic. At first what we did "felt good"—for the moment. I tried pushing my guilt into a closet and shutting the door, but kept on doing what came naturally. I remember thinking

even then, "What will you say to your daughter someday if she asks, 'Were you a virgin when you got married?'" Over the years that question has come to mind time and time again.

That day before the wedding my fiancé forced himself on me, and never having said no before, I felt helpless to stop him. All these years later I still feel the hurt and violation of that moment. There was no tenderness, no love, only desire, lust, passion.

How could I have known the repercussions through the years of that one decision on my part to have my own way and not God's? I realize what a precious, holy gift we so thoughtlessly threw away in our youth. And now I have had to ask my daughter, "Are you pregnant?" and hear her tearful reply, "Yes." I cannot express in words the deep wound to my soul this has caused. Although I did not make her decisions for her, I see that by my actions and choices so many years ago I left her spiritually vulnerable to Satan's onslaught.

If only I could look each teenage girl in the eye and tell her, "There are consequences to every moral decision you make; there are repercussions that will follow you the rest of your life and into the next generation!"

How I yearn to look each teenage boy in the eye and tell him, "Be strong. Be a real man.

Trust God's Word, discipline yourself, don't give in to youthful lust and trade your birthright of godly love for a mess of pottage that will turn to ashes in your heart."

I have learned too late the truth I heard a man of God say: "Love can always wait to give. Lust can never wait to get."

And you know—it's funny (sad) not a single time did those solemn moments of passion and lust bring real pleasure to me, either physically or emotionally.[2]

Such a story can be contrasted by stories of true love that are fostered by faithfulness to vows of purity. Columbia International University President Robertson McQuilkin found himself in an unusual situation when his lovely and gifted wife began to show the symptoms of Alzheimer's disease. She was a gifted hostess, an artist, a speaker in a morning radio program, a noted conference speaker, and an incredible helpmate to her husband.

When it became clear that Muriel needed his care, at the young age of fifty-seven President McQuilkin stepped down from his position to fulfill his responsibility. His words were, "She is such a delight to me. I don't have to care for her. I get to."[3]

This does not mean that it was without

struggle—like getting her to eat or bathe when she defiantly refused . . . or the past recreational grocery shopping together that was now different as she frequently loaded other people's carts and took off with them.

Resignation from his fruitful public ministry as president of a prestigious Christian university was also painful after being connected to it for twenty-four years. It was his vow that enabled him to make the decision. He stated, "Had I not promised, 42 years before, 'in sickness and in health . . . till death do us part'?" He had not forgotten her care and marvelous devotion to him in the previous four decades. Even in her difficult days, he extolled, "As I watch her brave descent into oblivion, Muriel is the joy of my life. Daily I discern new manifestation of the kind of person she is, the wife I always loved. I also see fresh manifestations of God's love—the God I long to love more fully."[4]

After McQuilkin cared for Muriel and watched her suffer from Alzheimer's for twenty-five years, the Lord took her home on September 20, 2003. As he reflected on what he had learned, he noted that it was painful to love her and know that she was not capable of loving him back. One day he thought, "Lord, is that the way it is between you and me? You pouring out your love and care so consciously, and what do you get back—a brief salute in the morning, we connect, grumbling when I don't get what I want, when you don't do it the way I like?"[5] McQuilkin has inspired countess others by his love and faithfulness to his vows.

Any failure can be placed under the precious blood of Christ. In the words of Joel 2:25, God is able to restore to us the years the locusts have eaten. The locusts were the form of God's discipline in the context of Joel's warning. God will honor a repentant heart, but we need to decisively deal with the issue. Get rid of the wrong relationship, the wrong peer group, or anything that is hindering your life. Today, place yourself in the arms of Christ and vow to be a one-man woman or a one-woman man.

11

PONDERING
A NEW
DIRECTION

IS THERE A WAY to avoid the heartaches of breakups, the emotional roller-coaster ride of relationships and premature physical and emotional attachment to the opposite sex? The pressure of hormones as well as the desire for peer acceptance is very strong and can push many in the wrong direction. Is dating God's way of preparing one for marriage, or could it possibly be something entirely contrary to marriage preparation? As many have said, "Breaking up is hard to do, but the more you do it, the easier it gets." In this sense, dating can be a preparation for divorce. Is there not a vast difference in "I love you until someone better comes along" and "I'm committed to you for a lifetime"?

We cannot dictate how this needs to work out in everyone's life. What is clear is that God does command each of us to guard our hearts with all diligence (Proverbs 4:23). This involves not only keeping ourselves physically for our mates but also emotionally. It is possible to not only be physically promiscuous but also emotionally promiscuous. Without a guarded heart our focus can easily shift from the Lord to seeking a mate and taking this matter into our own hands.

The best preparation for marriage is to maximize the use of the single years for the Lord. Our focus can be on becoming the person God desires us to be and developing life skills, as well as godly friendships. Such an approach maximizes the potential for pure friendships because the standard is "attention to all but intention toward none." In Christ, believers are able to treat each other with the purity of a brother-sister relationship, desiring each other's best in every way.

Using the family as a context for developing healthy relationships is a wise choice. As young people present their lives to the Lord with vows to preserve themselves for their life partner, they can respond to the Lord when they sense a freedom from their parents to pursue a relationship. In this model, the father assumes the responsibility to protect his children from a wrong marriage, to teach them God's truth, and to pray for the Lord to lead a future mate into their lives. This is not to be an attempt to control the children but simply to shepherd and guide them.

The father of the daughter gives his blessing to the young man to pursue his daughter. If a gal does not have a father, the family can choose a godly man who is willing to assume this role. God will honor the heart of anyone who desires His best, and He will work with anyone who is surrendered to Him regardless of circumstances. I read of one father who gave a heart-shaped pendant to his daughter. The pendant had a small keyhole and an accompanying key. The father held the key as a symbol that her heart was given to him. When the father gave permission to the young man to court his daughter, he gave the key to the courter.

There is a great advantage in getting to know one another's families. I had the privilege of living with my fiancée's family during our engagement. A courtship activity could even be going on a family mission trip! The important thing is to seek the Lord and not a formula or a method.[1]

We might summarize the principles we have examined in the following ways:

- Be committed to keep yourself sexually pure for the mate who is God's will for you.
- Be committed to guard your heart, focusing on loving the Lord and serving Him.
- Be committed to pursue lasting and pure friendships.
- Be committed to concentrate on your preparations for life and ministry without the distraction of seeking premature emotional relationships.
- Be committed to honor the family structure and accept family counsel in regard to a potential marriage partner.
- Be committed to keep yourself pure in mind and body.
- Be committed to pursue love and not lust.

When such commitments are rightly motivated, they can remove ungodly pressure from our lives. The pressure for a fellow to impress a girl with an expensive car, flashy clothes, and other means can be removed so he can use his energy to pursue the Lord and a life of true love. A girl's energy can be shifted away from expensive makeup, sensual clothes, and ungodly flattery to the development of godly character that can benefit many future generations to do God's will. The pressure to engage in a "big search" to find a potential lover can be placed in the hands of God and aided by mature godly people.

A person might even write down qualities that he believes the most important in marriage. Parents could even encourage their children to do this. This can be the beginning of developing discernment at a young age of what are the most essential elements in a marriage relationship. Parents can even work through some of the questions in appendix one with a child as an educational tool. Certainly, a single adult can benefit from looking at these issues before emotions make it hard to think clearly.

The focus of such contemplation is not primarily to develop a checklist with which to scrutinize potential marriage partners. It is rather to develop a heart that esteems and values things that God esteems. A physical attraction to another person is a factor to be considered, but one must realize that in thirty years the other person will look different. However, the qualities of diligence, gratefulness, faithfulness, sensitivity, gentleness, and reverence will become only more attractive as one ages.

It is not only wrong values that bog people down in this area of waiting on God for marriage. There can be a self-centered avoidance of marriage that is connected to the subtle desire to extend one's adolescence and not grow up to be a responsible adult. This is far different than using one's single years to serve the Lord.

You are blessed if you have friends who can help you assess and develop Christlike character. It also helpful to realize that your present family relationships can set patterns that could affect a marriage. Would you desire to marry a person like yourself? What will you be like as a marriage partner? The way a young man treats his mother and sister tends to set the tone for how he will treat his future wife. In a similar vein, a young lady's relationship to her father and brothers can establish set ways of relating to her future husband.

It is right for a parent to seek to raise a boy to be ready to protect a wife, provide for a family, and cherish a woman. It is right for a parent to seek to raise a girl to have the godly character it takes to be a loving wife and mother in God's will. It is right for a godly adult single to trust God to build these qualities in his or her life. God will use good character to bless others whatever His will is for us in regard to marriage.

If this whole process of contemplating marriage encourages you to seek God and love Him with your whole heart, you are doing it the right way. Appeal to God for His mercy to build in you all that you need to be successful in His eyes for His will concerning marriage. The apostle Paul credited God's mercy with transforming him from a murderer into a trustworthy man (1 Corinthians 7:25). God can do the same for us!

12

HANDLING
YOUR PASSIONS

"CAN I WAIT ON GOD in light of the raging desire within me for intimacy?" is an honest question. What is the answer for a believer in Christ in regard to his or her sex life? When a person becomes a Christian, he does not lose his sex appeal or sexual appetite. The answer is not found in ignoring or suppressing what God has clearly created within us. We should bring this matter into the very presence of God and thank Him for His design.

Let us first review some of the things we have already discovered:

- Only the Cross can miraculously deliver us from living a self-focused life. Christ alone can release us to live for a purpose bigger than ourselves (2 Corinthians 5:14–15).
- Only the Lord can train us to be content in our circumstances and to utilize our years to the fullest (Philippians 4:11–13; 1 Corinthians 7:32–35).
- As we specifically present our sexual energies and drives to God and vow to keep ourselves pure for one person, God will send His support from heaven day by day and moment by moment.

We will be tempted sexually. Life is a battle, and, as I have said, some days will be more difficult than others. The Bible says that "the days are evil" (Ephesians 5:16). There are some days that your goal may be just to make it through the day! I will give you a few suggestions that hopefully will be of some help.

God yearns to share His wisdom with us, and our trials and temptations can create in us a hunger for His answers. The Christian life is to be lived each moment in complete dependence upon the Holy Spirit (Ephesians 5:17–21; Galatians 5:16). This is the only way to live the life that God has called us to live.

In the beginning of my almost seven-year

wait after meeting the one whom God had for me, I was very discouraged because of her lack of response. In one of my most discouraging days, the Lord laid on my heart a vision of putting His Word in my life. I believe that God gave me the idea of a twenty-year goal to study and meditate on His Word.

There are 31,173 verses in my Bible. This used to be a meaningless statistic until I saw how it could help me. I decided to study a certain number of verses a week. Even allowing for one day off each week and two weeks off each year, I could make it through the Bible in twenty years.

I still use and review the notes from this twenty-year project. The first seven years of it were the last seven years of my single life. I would not have been able to do it with the same effectiveness if I had been married at that time. I would have not been as hungry for it had I not been so discouraged.

Let your battles and discouragement drive you to God to find His plans and dreams for you today! Do not let it drive you to an attempt to relieve your personal pain with sexual pleasure that will rob you of true fulfillment and also bring great dishonor to your loving Lord.

At any stage of life God has new things that He wants to do in your life. After John Naber

won five gold medals for his swimming in the
1976 Olympics in Montreal, something very
startling happened to him. He became deeply
depressed after returning home and going
through all the interviews by the press. He had
lived with a single-minded focus: to win these
gold medals. Now that he had accomplished
this, he realized that he did not have any other
goals. As he began to reset new goals of how he
might serve Christ, the Lord met him at his
point of need. Whatever your present point of
need, the Lord desires to meet you. Ask Him for
His goals for you.

Another suggestion is to deal with any rebellion in your life. The Christian life is a spiritual battle, and the only way to exercise our
spiritual authority is to be under the Lord's authority (James 4:7). A young person who was
unsuccessfully battling his sensual lust asked
for advice. As I got to know his heart, I discovered another problem—his rebellion against
the authority of his parents. He said, "I'm not
coming to you for that."

My reply was, "Unless you deal with that,
you will never be victorious in your other concerns." When any of us is not under the authority of God—and this includes submission
to His appointed human authorities in our lives

—we will lose spiritual battles that God never intended us to lose.

When you put one area of your life under the control of God, it has a positive effect on other areas. In this sense discipline can be contagious, but the opposite can also be true. If eating is out of control, usually the thought life is as well.

I remember a dear Christlike young man humbly sharing with me the two things that enabled him to put his sexual drives under God's control. One was to deal with the rebellion in his heart and place himself under the authority of his parents. The second was to begin to incorporate the discipline of fasting in his life.[1]

All areas of one's life need to be placed under the loving control of the Spirit, allowing Him to produce self-control in us. This can be true for such areas as our sleep. Many of us can testify that when we fail to obey God's prompting to arise and slothfully lie in bed, our minds can succumb to temptation. Even the area of physical exercise needs to be surrendered to God so that He can lead us in utilizing this helpful discipline. Physical exercise is not the most important thing, but it can be an aid in putting drives under God's control.

C. S. Lewis alluded to these matters when he wrote:

Good and evil both increase at compound interest, that is why the little decisions you and I make every day are of such infinite importance. The smallest good act today is the capture of a strategic point from which, a few months later, you will be able to go on to victories you never dreamed of. An apparent trivial indulgence in lust or anger today is the loss of a ridge or railway line or bridgehead from which the enemy may launch an attack otherwise impossible.[2]

We are not to try and fight this battle alone. We need the help of other pure-hearted friends to aid us and keep us accountable. We need people with whom we can walk in the light in honesty, openness, and transparency. Author Ed Welch suggests these seven questions that can be used in accountability relationships:

1. Have you been with a woman anywhere this past week that might be seen as compromising?
2. Have any of your financial dealings lacked integrity?
3. Have you exposed yourself to any sexually explicit material?
4. Have you spent adequate time in Bible study and prayer?

5. Have you given priority time to your family?
6. Have you fulfilled the mandates of your calling?
7. Have you just lied to me?[3]

In a survey on sexuality, which *U.S. News and World Report* called the "most authoritative ever," it was found that not only was sex better in marriage, but it was best if you had only one sexual partner in a lifetime.[4] Other research has shown that not only are married people better off than those who simply live together, but also that marriages that are preceded by cohabitation are 50 to 100 percent more likely to end in divorce.[5]

God desires us to live in His wise and good ways. In order to do this, we need to humble ourselves and receive the aid of God that often comes from His people. We will have needs to both give and receive love. This is even greater than our desire for physical intimacy. If we have spiritual intimacy with Christ and loving relationships, it is possible to bear not having physical intimacy. When the loving relationships with the Lord and others are missing, the physical drive can be an unbearable temptation.

DISCERNING
GOD'S WILL

IS THIS HIS PERSON AND HIS TIMING?

I RECEIVED an encouraging letter in the mail from a former student named Susan:

> *I'm now forty-four years old and God has given me great contentment, joy, faith, and knowledge in His love. You once suggested praying for a man with the qualities in Psalm 112. I've also added James 3:17–18 to that list! My prayer request to you one semester was for a husband. Well, God has brought me a wonderful Christian man following a forty-day fasting period at*

*my church last spring. Both of us had partici-
pated in the fast and had never spoken much be-
yond "hello" before.*

She talked about meeting him on a Sunday
afternoon at a friend's house and talking for
hours. They began to spend time together with
her pastor and his wife as accountability partners. "With God's continued blessing, we plan
to be engaged and married this year," she wrote!
Her letter continued:

*God's goodness, mercy, wisdom, and kind-
ness are so great! You once told us that when
God has something amazing to do, He will usually have us wait for it. That has so encouraged
me through the past few years. The Lord has
blessed us abundantly more than we would ask
or imagine according to His power working in
us! My many prayers of the past ten years (since
I received Christ), all these little things, special
qualities I've prayed for, are so miraculously apparent in Charlie. Keep encouraging single
adults like me to pray specifically, trust completely, and obey faithfully.*

The delight in Susan's heart was the result of
waiting on God for His person and His timing
in her life. Let us examine three crucial ques-

tions that may be helpful in discerning whether or not you have been led to God's person and is it His timing.

DOES IT FIT IN WITH GOD'S PRESENT AGENDA FOR YOUR LIFE?

I sensed God leading me to do further schooling after completing graduate school. While I was talking to a noted theologian who headed up a doctoral program of a well-known seminary, he said, "If you are considering doctoral work, you might consider staying single a few more years." I think he was almost surprised that he had said it. He told me not to let his comments unduly restrain me from developing a relationship, but he was attempting to give me some fatherly advice. The week before, he had to encourage a married man to drop out of his doctoral studies because his marriage was being neglected.

This proved to be God's counsel for me. Marriage did not fit into God's agenda at this time. I did pursue doctoral studies, and it was God's will for me to complete these while I was single.

There are things that God desires to do in us and through us that can be more effectively accomplished during our single years. During this time, devote your attention toward a growing relationship with the Lord. Let Him mold you.

What if all you know is a broken family pattern, from which you are merely a refugee who survived? The years of singleness are an opportunity to transplant yourself into fields where you can grow in knowing God, in knowing yourself as you unfold the pain of your past before the Lord and His people, and in expanding the journey of your heart within loving relationships. Before the Lord, commit your single years to personal learning and growth.

C. S. Lewis once said, "We read to know that we are not alone." Courage and inspiration for the journey often comes in the packages of other people who have gone before us. Let God dig deep in your soul and confront your anger, fears, pride, and unresolved conflicts. No one will ever enter marriage perfect, but a failure to acknowledge and then to deal with soul issues can greatly hinder any close relationship.

DO YOU HAVE THE BLESSING OF YOUR PARENTS?

The bride and groom are ultimately responsible to make their decisions before the Lord. While on one extreme it might be unwise to marry someone for the sole purpose of satisfying one's parents, it would be equally unwise not to honor them by carefully weighing their advice and cautions.

Yesterday I talked to one dear young man who waited one year for his parents-in-law's blessing. The reason that it was being withheld was his career path. He desired to follow God's call to be a pastor, but the father of the girl desired him to come work in his business and receive a lucrative salary. As he observed the genuine character of the young man for over a year, he gave his blessing for them to be married. Such a wait was helpful in his relationship with his father-in-law, who began to open his heart to spiritual truth. It also was a great relief for his wife to enter the marriage under the blessings of both her parents.

I have observed some amazing things as people have trusted God to work through their God-given authorities. One dear colleague that I teach with is a Jewish Christian. After an almost five-year wait because of their objections to marrying somebody who was not Jewish, his Jewish parents told him to marry that nice Gentile girl! There is fruit when others can not only hear the gospel but also see it at work through submissive and respectful lives.

One day a girl came up to me and talked about a relationship with a fellow whom she desired to marry. Her parents were not yet convinced at this point. I asked her to consider these four questions as she evaluated her relationship before the Lord:

1. Do you have a clear conscience toward your parents in regard to your attitudes and your actions? Look for such things as a disloyal spirit, a self-righteousness attitude, or an ungrateful heart. Any of these can greatly spoil any marriage.

2. Have you asked your parents/godly mentor(s) to point out your blind spots? God may clearly be trying to protect you from something you cannot see.

   One of the sweetest Christian girls I have ever known was a girl I met in college. She had an incredible heart for God, and I admired her life. We did spend some time together, and I did wonder if this was God's person for me. My mother, in a very uncharacteristic way, one day said that it would not be best in any way. I did honor her advice and now can see very clearly where she was coming from. It would not at all have been a good "fit." There was certainly nothing wrong with the girl, herself. We probably were just not the right balance, and God had different people for both of us and more single years for me before marriage.

In other areas, my parents have seen things that I did not. I so desired to go right into ministry following college. They strongly encouraged me to get seminary training, which was indeed God's will for me in order to fulfill His calling for my life. I did not like their advice at the time, but God used them to help me make a wise decision.

3. Have you explained your personal convictions to your parents without a spirit of condemnation? It may be that you have a spiritual frame of reference that your parents do not have. Rest assured that God is a big God who ultimately controls all authority (Proverbs 21:1).

   A person I mentioned earlier told his future father-in-law in a very meek way that God had called him to be a pastor. He respectfully declined the lucrative business offer. In so doing, he did what God called him to do but without unnecessary offense. It is one thing for the gospel to be an offense but quite another for our arrogant selves to be the cause of offense.

4. Have you given God time to change your authority's mind? A couple I saw last week was one that I had counseled over ten years ago.

I strongly encouraged them to not marry after the girl's freshman's year. I did not realize until many years later that they did indeed wait. They had been counseled by another person and the father of the bride to also wait. They got married in God's timing, and now they are experiencing His blessings as they prepare to go to the mission field.

ARE YOU FINANCIALLY AND VOCATIONALLY READY FOR MARRIAGE?

God does put the responsibility on the husband to provide (1 Timothy 5:8). The man should ask himself if he is able to provide at a level at which his future wife would be content. Also, if, for instance, the girl is used to a luxurious lifestyle, has she considered the implications of living with someone who may not be able to provide that?

God gave Adam a mission to obey Him, and then He provided a helper in Eve. The provision came right after the command (Genesis 2:16–18). The context would indicate that a wife is God's provision to help a husband to obey Him. The focus of the single years is to discover God's calling, and then obey Him. If a man needs a wife to fulfill this calling, he can surely believe God to provide one in His timing.

All believers are viewed as a precious gift that the Father has given to the Son (John 17:24). When God draws two people together, a godly wife is also described as a gift of God to the man (Proverbs 19:14). The word "helper" in Genesis 2:18 is in no means a degrading term because God Himself is described in Scripture in this way (Hebrews 13:6). In fact, it means supplying what the other is incapable of supplying for himself.

The Greek translation of the Old Testament known as the Septuagint translates "helper" with a Greek word, *boethos,* that is used in the New Testament in the sense of physician. It conveys an idea of being able to assist and aid another who is oppressed and in need. A look at the verb form of this word provides some interesting insight in regard to specific help:

Help in spiritual warfare (Matthew 15:25;
    Mark 9:27)
Help in battle with doubts (Mark 9:24)
Help in doing God's work (Acts 16:9)

The godly woman also has the right to ask the man, "What do you want me to help you do?" In other words, if the man is seeking to find his fulfillment in her alone and has no direction, is this the man to whom she would desire to give her life? Before a girl should consider marrying a man she should ask herself:

- Am I willing to submit to his leadership?
- Do I have a growing respect for him?
- Do I sense God's love for me through him?
- Could I live with him the rest of my life on earth?

Remember that God has a greater concern for your life partner than you do! You can count on Him to prepare you for your mate and your mate for you. You can trust Him to enable you to find and recognize each other. He knows how to bring two people together. When it is of the Lord, then the two of you will "fit" together, having a harmony of spirit.[1] This means that both of your spirits have been made alive or regenerated. It also means that the presence of the other person should invigorate you spiritually to obey God. If you do not start with spiritual harmony, the relationship will never be what God intended it to be.

Compatibility in your souls or personalities is needed as well. It does not mean you are identical or even similar, but it does mean that you can complement each other mentally and socially.

There will also be a harmony in regard to

physical makeup. There are no immutable laws in regard to physical harmony, but there will be some kind of compatibility acceptable to the couple before the Lord in regard to age, health, and physical features.

To say there is harmony or affinity in spirit, soul, and body does not mean that there are no continual adjustments. It does mean that as the couple continually responds to the Lord's working in their lives, they will experience true fellowship with each other. This is the fruit of "walking in the light" before God (1 John 1:7). As one walks openly, honestly, and transparently before the Lord and His truth, he can continually grow in oneness with Him and the key relationships of his life.

14

THE SECRET
OF WAITING

THE SECRET OF WAITING is something that Jesus has revealed to us. I saw the power of this truth one Sunday night when I was asked to speak to a group of singles at a suburban church in Chicago. I had just started teaching at Moody Bible Institute and was a twenty-eight-year-old single at that time. A young man in his thirties, full of anger and concern, came up to me afterward.

The young man came up to me with an open Bible. It was opened to a verse that he asked me to read. He pointed to Proverbs 5:18, which gives the command to rejoice in the wife of your youth. He said, "Look at me! I'm getting older and there is no wife in whom to rejoice." He was clearly angry with God for not providing him a wife. He said, "I go up to girls to share Christ with them, not because I care for their souls, but just because I desire to talk with them."

Anything I shared with this person only seemed to make him angrier. However, when I asked him the next question, a spirit of hope entered the room. "Do you think you could trust God to get you through the remainder of this day as a single man?"

"Oh, sure," he replied.

"That's all the faith you will ever have to have," I told him.

You can tackle any area of your life one moment at a time and one day at a time. It is Jesus who graciously commanded us not to be anxious for tomorrow (Matthew 6:34). When most of us think about trusting God with our singleness, we are not thinking of trusting Him for today. We are thinking about trusting Him for the days, weeks, months, and years potentially ahead. Faith always has to be living in the present. God does not give us the grace today to deal with tomorrow's concerns. Any planning that needs to be made for the tomorrows of our lives must be done in the context of today's agenda.

As this angry man digested Jesus' wisdom, his anger was transformed into a peaceful trust.

As you wait and believe God one day at a time, do not hesitate to be open and honest with Him about your desires. Unburdening your heart in this way, with thankfulness to the Lord, is the road to peace (Philippians 4:6–7).

The only way that you are able to thank God in circumstances that you are not emotionally excited about is by coming to the conviction that God is both sovereign and good. God is better than your most ideal thought of any other delightful thing or person. If this were not true, He would be less than perfect.

God is not trying to squeeze something out of you in order to meet some need in His life. He is perfectly complete and desires you to know His fellowship that is restful for your soul (Matthew 11:28–30). His will is good, acceptable, and perfect (Romans 12:2). His will is exactly what you would desire if you knew all the facts.

Satan attacked Eve's understanding of God's goodness in the garden and led humanity into sin (Genesis 3:1–4). Every human faces this scheme of the devil each day of his life. Realize, too, that some of God's good gifts may come in strange packages. It is not often that you hear someone thanking God for the good gift of loneliness. However, it is often in loneliness that the deepest companionship with God is cultivated. Anything that encourages you to cry out to God can be overruled for good. As long as you seek God, He can put His prospering hand upon you to fulfill His will (2 Chronicles 26:5).

God's ways are good. To seek the primary thing also leads to the experience of the secondary things. This is what Jesus taught in Matthew 6:33:

> *But seek first His kingdom and His righteousness, and all these things will be added to you.*

It is also what the psalmist taught in Psalm 37:4 and 84:11:

> *Delight yourself in the Lord;*
> *And He will give you the desires of your heart.*

> *For the Lord God is a sun and shield;*
> *The Lord gives grace and glory;*
> *No good thing does He withhold from those who walk uprightly.*

It is our daily responsibility to delight in the Lord and walk uprightly. It is God's responsibility to give us the good things. And God does say, "He who finds a wife finds a good thing"

(Proverbs 18:22). God's will is in harmony with your deepest desires and what will bring you the greatest eternal good. It is my earnest prayer for you that our wonderful Lord would bless you abundantly as you look to Him to satisfy every thirst of your heart.

> *"If anyone is thirsty, let him come to Me and drink.* (John 7:37)

As Ravi Zacharias has said, "Based on what you know, trust God for what you do not know." And, remember, you only have to trust Him one day at a time!

NOTES

Chapter 2: Waiting on God for a Mate

1. Tim Kimmel, *Legacy of Love* (Portland, Oreg.: Mult-nomah, 1989), 165–66.
2. Helen Kooiman, *Silhouttes: Women Behind Great Men* (Waco, Tex.: Word, 1972), 22–24.

Chapter 3: Finding God's Provision on the Other Side of a Temptation

1. Bill Thrasher, *Living the Life God Has Planned* (Chicago: Moody, 2001), 175–87.
2. Ibid, 62–66.

Chapter 8: Developing a Conviction Before God

1. See Bill Thrasher, *Journey to Victorious Praying* (Chicago: Moody, 2003), 163–175, for how to wait and what to do as you wait.

2. Jeremiah Burroughs, *The Rare Jewel of Christian Contentment* (Edinburgh: Banner Truth Trust, 1979).

Chapter 9: Discovering the Secret of Contentment

1. Consult Thrasher, *Journey to Victorious Praying*, 17–38, for ideas about how to respond to temptation.

Chapter 10: Making an Important Commitment

1. David A. Seamonds, *Living with Your Dreams* (Wheaton: Victor, 1990).

2. Elizabeth Elliott, "Is He a God of Love?" *The Elisabeth Elliot Newsletter*, September/October 1998, 2.

3. Robertson McQuilkin, "Living by Vows," *Christianity Today*, 8 October 1990.

4. Ibid.

5. Robertson McQuilkin, as quoted in an interview with Stan Guthrie, "The Gradual Grief of Alzheimer's," *Christianity Today*, February 2004, 64.

Chapter 11: Pondering a New Direction

1. For more reading in this area consider:

Elisabeth Elliot, *Passion and Purity*, 2nd ed. (Grand Rapids: Revel, 2002).

Martha Ruppert, *The Dating Trap* (Chicago: Moody, 2000).

Chapter 12: Handling Your Passions

1. For how to get started on fasting, see Thrasher, *Journey to Victorious Praying*, 141–60.

2. Taken from the C. S. Lewis Foundation Web site: www.cslewis.org.

3. Edward T. Welch, *When People Are Big and God Is Small* (Phillipsburg, N.J.: P & R Publishing, 1997), 204.

4. Robert T. Michael, John H. Gagnon, Edward O. Laumann, and Gina Bari Kolata. *Sex in America: A Definitive Survey* (Boston: Little, Brown, & Co., 1994), 124.

5. William Axinn and Arlann Thornton, "The Relationship Between Cohabitation and Divorce: Selectively or Causal Influence," *Demography* 29 (1992): 358.

Chapter 13: Discerning God's Will

1. See appendix 1 for further resources.

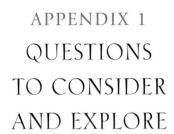

APPENDIX 1

QUESTIONS
TO CONSIDER
AND EXPLORE

QUESTIONS TO CONSIDER TO CONFIRM
YOUR DECISION TO MARRY

1. How do you think that you and your prospective mate can better serve and obey God together than separately? Are you both obeying God now? Do you have a clear conscience in your relationship with each other?

2. Can you describe at least three positive and at least three negative characteristics of your prospective bride or groom?

3. Can you give three reasons why you think this is the person you should marry?

4. Can you give three reasons why you think this is the right time for you to marry?

5. Go to each of your parents and ask, "What do you think each of us needs to work on in order to have a successful marriage?"

6. Do you have a clear conscience toward your parents?

7. How do you feel your personalities complement each other and conflict with each other? Consider taking the Taylor Johnson Temperament analysis or the MBTI® (Myers-Briggs Type Indicator).

8. Are you able to praise the other person in public?

9. What fears and anxieties do you have about marrying this person? Have you shared them with your parents, with your spiritual leaders, and with your prospective mate?

10. Are you able to disagree with your prospective mate without getting angry? How do you handle your anger?

11. Have you made out a budget to consider the financial obligation of marriage?

12. Have you read any books on Christian marriage and parenting?

13. Do you feel your future partner is a one-man woman or a one-woman man?

14. Are you able to communicate on a spiritual level with this person? Do you enjoy his or her company and conversation?

15. How is this relationship different than others you may have had before?

QUESTIONS TO EXPLORE TOGETHER TO PROVIDE A FOUNDATION FOR MARRIAGE DURING ENGAGEMENT

1. Have you examined the passages that explain the roles of a husband and a wife? (See Ephesians 5:22–33; Colossians 3:18–19; 1 Peter 3:1–7; Titus 2:3–5; Genesis 2:18-24.)

2. Are you prepared to vow to God to fulfill these commands? (See sample vows in the next appendix.)

3. List practical ways that you plan to fulfill each of these responsibilities (e.g., Wife: submit, respect, love; Husband: love, nourish, cherish, grant honor, live with understanding).

4. How would you like your marriage to be like that of your parents?

5. In what ways would you like to parent like your parents did?

6. List your thoughts and expectations about the following areas. Do it independently and then share it with your fiancé(e).

a. Finances: Who will make financial decisions? Will you go in debt? Will the wife work outside the home? How do you plan to use a budget? What part of your income will be given to the Lord? Who will determine how the money is spent?

b. Children: What are your convictions about family planning? How many children do you desire? How soon would you like children? What do you believe about the disciplining of children? Who should take responsibility for educating and training them?

c. Outside friends, hobbies, and entertainment: What would you expect to pursue independent of your mate? What would you expect your mate not to do without you?

d. Divorce: Do you think this marriage could be terminated under any circumstances?

e. Parents: Where do you plan to spend your holidays or vacations? How much time do you feel you should spend with your parents and in-laws in the first year of your marriage?

f. Church: Where do you plan to go to church? How do you expect to have family and personal devotions?

g. Love and affection: Do you think your sexual needs are more or less than your fiancé(e)? Do you think your need for affection is more or less than your fiancé(e)? Do you think your need for praise and encouragement is more or less than your fiancé(e)? How do you think birthdays and special occasions should be celebrated?

h. Responsibilities at home: What do you expect to do? What do you expect your mate to do?

7. In what ways are you like your mate and in what ways are you different?

a. Organized or disorganized
b. Talkative or quiet
c. Prefers to stay home or go out on free evenings
d. Frugal or freely spends money
e. Procrastinates or "attacks" responsibilities
f. Early riser or night owl
g. Follower or leader

VOWS

GROOM'S VOW

I VOW BEFORE GOD and to you to love you as Christ loved the church—to give of myself for your eternal benefit. I will do all that He empowers me to do to protect, direct, provide, and purify you by God's Word that you might be fully available to the Lord on earth and one day presented to the Lord in heaven in a way that brings the greatest glory to God and the greatest eternal satisfaction to you.

I vow to love you as I love myself—as I seek to understand and apply all that it means to nourish and cherish you. I understand that any injury I do to you is also an injury to myself as God wills that we are one.

I will seek to live with you in an understanding manner and grant you honor and favor as an equal in every way, that our communication with God not be hindered.

If God wills to give us children, I will accept them as God's gift and seek to lovingly nourish and discipline them and to do all that He empowers me to do to win their complete hearts to the true and living God and our Lord Jesus Christ.

I will depend on God's merciful providence and His supporting, motivating, and enabling grace. Penny, the greatest human help in fulfilling these vows comes from your merciful love and support, which I readily and humbly say I deeply need. I believe God has called you and no one else to be my wife and helper.

You have already seen me fail in my God-given duty to love you as I should. I purpose to ask forgiveness at each point of failure and never to forget, as God never will, what I have vowed today.

Penny, I call upon God to detect, judge, and discipline any hindrance and all obstacles to fully experience the oneness that He has willed. Whether this hindrance be in my own attitude or action or in any outside person or force, I call upon God to deal with it and rest in the confidence, "What God has joined together, let no man separate," and "Since God is for us, who can be against us?" [Romans 8:31 NLV].

For God's glory and your eternal benefit, I pledge thee my faithfulness.

BRIDE'S VOW

God has created me to be your helpmate, and I know my greatest joy and fulfillment will come in working alongside of you as you seek to love God, to walk in His Spirit, and to love His world for His highest glory.

Knowing there can only be one head in our family, and God has ordained that the husband be the head of the wife, I vow to submit to you —to yield my will to yours and to seek to know your desires and to do them.

By God's grace I purpose to reverence you by respecting and highly esteeming you and your position before God. I have already had the joy of experiencing your wise and loving leadership, and I will look to you for my direction.

You have also seen me fail, and I purpose to ask your forgiveness and seek restoration and the oneness of spirit we both treasure. If God should bless us with children, I purpose to work with you in prayerfully nurturing them to love our Lord Jesus Christ and to walk in His ways.

Bill, I deeply need you. You are the Psalm 112 man that I have prayed for to be my husband. I am so thankful for such a godly man who seeks the Lord with a whole heart. God has done exceeding abundantly above all that I could ask or think in giving me you and you alone to be my husband. It is with great joy that I vow to tenderly love you and not to depart from you all the days of my life, and thereto I pledge you my faithfulness.

STUDY GUIDE

1. How do you react to the words of Charles Simeon in regard to his singleness?
2. List all the benefits of singleness that you can see in 1 Corinthians 7.
3. If you are single, what specific things are you able to do in your present state to seek and serve Christ?
4. How do you balance the teaching of 1 Corinthians 7 with Proverbs 5:18?

CHAPTER TWO
WAITING ON GOD FOR A MATE

1. List all the principles that you can learn from Genesis 2 about marriage.

CHAPTER THREE
FINDING GOD'S PROVISION ON
THE OTHER SIDE OF A TEMPTATION

1. What do you think are some of the most important preparations for marriage?
2. What times are the most challenging for you to be content in your marital status?
3. Look at Matthew 4:1–11. How was Jesus tempted to take matters in His own hands with each of the three recorded temptations?
4. How can a person take the matter of pursuing a marriage partner into his or her own hands?

CHAPTER FOUR
REPENTING OF IDOLATRY AFTER
EXPERIENCING LOVE AT FIRST SIGHT

1. What factors can influence a wrong first impression of a person?

2. What do you do if you have an attraction to someone who is not free to respond to you?
3. How do you know when another person has become an "idol" in your life?

CHAPTER FIVE
REBIRTH OF THE VISION:
PURIFY MY HEART AMIDST CLOSED DOORS

1. What can help you to have a pure interest in someone you are attracted to?

CHAPTER SIX
EXPERIENCING GOD'S PROVIDENCE
AND DELAYED ANSWERS TO PRAYERS

1. In what way is a broken heart a key preparation for ministry?
2. What would you say if someone asked you, "At the end of your life what would you like to have accomplished?"
3. Why is it not wise to try to handle alone the area of waiting on God for a mate? How can others help?
4. What is the difference between resting in another person's love and feeling you have to perform for it?

CHAPTER SEVEN
LEARNING FROM THE OTHER SIDE OF THE STORY

1. Discuss what the prayer of Exodus 33:15 means in regard to your pursuits: "If Your presence does not go with us, do not lead us up from here."
2. How can you relate to your life the idea of being asked to yield up to God your most prized relationship, as God required Abraham to do with Isaac?

CHAPTER EIGHT
DEVELOPING A CONVICTION BEFORE GOD

1. How do you sense God desires to use your singleness as you wait on Him for His will in regard to marriage?
2. When are special times of temptation that you feel very alone? Discuss how to prepare for these times and commit them to the Lord.

CHAPTER NINE
DISCOVERING THE SECRET OF CONTENTMENT

1. Discuss what Paul terms as the "secret" of contentment.

2. Discuss the promise of 1 Corinthians 3:21–23 and ask God to make it real to you.
3. What attributes of God are especially helpful when you battle discontentment?
4. What does it mean to delight in the Lord?
5. What is your greatest threat of idolatry, and how does God want you to respond?
6. Mention the people whom you have met that exhibit a godly contentment.

CHAPTER TEN
MAKING AN IMPORTANT COMMITMENT

1. How can you do your mate good even before you know who he or she is (Proverbs 31:12)?
2. Prayerfully consider making a vow to be a one-man woman or a one-woman man.
3. Write to the Lord and your future mate, and tell them about your desire to preserve your life for them.
4. If you are not certain of complete forgiveness for any past moral failure, seek God and get the help of a godly, mature Christian.

CHAPTER ELEVEN
PONDERING A NEW DIRECTION

1. Write out your convictions about courtship or "dating," and discuss them with your friends.
2. Whose guidance should be considered for developing relationships with the opposite sex that might lead to marriage?
3. Discuss character qualities of a man and of a woman that provide the foundation for a "successful" life and marriage.

CHAPTER TWELVE
HANDLING YOUR PASSIONS

1. Ask the Lord what goals He has for your present single years. Write them down.
2. Examine your relationship with your God-appointed authorities, and ask the Lord to show you any lack of submission.
3. What areas of your life need to be brought under God's control (e.g., eating, sleeping, exercise, etc.)?
4. Discuss how the Lord might begin to use the discipline of fasting in your life.
5. What are your plans for personal accountability?

CHAPTER THIRTEEN
DISCERNING GOD'S WILL

1. How can one discern God's will in regard to the timing and the person for a marriage partner?
2. What does it means to have an affinity of spirit with another person? An affinity of soul? A physical affinity?

CHAPTER FOURTEEN
THE SECRET OF WAITING

1. What does it look like to live one day at a time and not be anxious for tomorrow?
2. What lies from Satan, the world, and the flesh attack your understanding of God's goodness?
3. How do verses like Matthew 6:33 and Psalm 37:4 and 84:11 reflect God's goodness?

ABOUT THE AUTHOR

Bill Thrasher is a professor of Bible and Theology in the graduate school of the Moody Bible Institute. He and his wife, Penny, live in Wheaton. Bill is the author of *A Journey to Victorious Praying* and *Living the Life God Has Planned.*

More from Dr. Bill Thrasher

A Journey to Victorious Praying

A Journey to Victorious Praying *is wide-ranging in conception, refreshingly biblical, and ever practical. Bill Thrasher has mined the Scriptures and the literature of prayer to give us a volume that will change lives. I sense that he did this magnificent work on his knees.*

R. Kent Hughes,
Senior Pastor,
College Church,
Wheaton

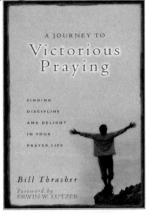

ISBN: 0-8024-3698-6

Living the Life God Has Planned

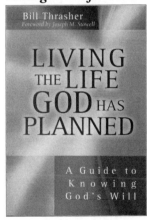

ISBN: 0-8024-3699-4

When we come to know God's wondrous attributes and His flawless character, we can set about living the life He intended. In this rich and bountiful book, Bill Thrasher unveils the key to living in the center of God's will. By focusing on God's character, we are aligned with His will. When we learn to abide in Him, to take all of our needs and frustrations to Him, everything falls into place.

MOODY
PUBLISHERS

THE NAME YOU CAN TRUST®

1-800-678-6928 www.MoodyPublishers.org

SINCE 1894, Moody Publishers has been dedicated to equip and motivate people to advance the cause of Christ by publishing evangelical Christian literature and other media for all ages, around the world. Because we are a ministry of the Moody Bible Institute of Chicago, a portion of the proceeds from the sale of this book go to train the next generation of Christian leaders.

If we may serve you in any way in your spiritual journey toward understanding Christ and the Christian life, please contact us at www.moodypublishers.com.

"All Scripture is God-breathed and is useful for teaching, rebuking, correcting and training in righteousness, so that the man of God may be thoroughly equipped for every good work."
—2 TIMOTHY 3:16, 17

MOODY
PUBLISHERS

THE NAME YOU CAN TRUST®

BELIEVING GOD FOR HIS BEST TEAM

ACQUIRING EDITOR
Greg Thornton

COPY EDITOR
Ali Childers

BACK COVER COPY
Lisa Cockrel

COVER DESIGN
Ragont Design

INTERIOR DESIGN
Ragont Design

PRINTING AND BINDING
Versa Press, Inc.

The typeface for the text of this book is
Giovanni